D1241008

What if George Bush were.....

A Black Man?

Dr. Boyce D. Watkins

Blue Boy Publishing Co.
Camillus, NY.

Copyright © 2005 by Dr. Boyce Watkins
All rights reserved.

Published by

Blue Boy Publishing Co.
PO Box 691
Camillus, NY. 13031 – 0691

Printed in the United States of America
Cover designed by Linda Pratt

First printing, July, 2004

Library of Congress Catalogue-in-
Publications Data

What if George Bush were a Black Man?, 1st
ed.

p.cm.

ISBN: 0-9742632-2-2
Library of Congress Control Number:
2005933430

Disclaimer

All statements made in this book are matters of social commentary and opinion. All facts stated are verified with the most reliable sources available. Neither the author nor the publisher assume responsibility for errors.

Dedication

To my daughter Patrice. This is also dedicated to Charles, Donald, Felicia, Lakisha, Larry, Latanja, Lawrence, Robin, Thaiiesha, and Valeria.

I would also like to thank George Bush, Bill Cosby, Bob Johnson, Michael Moore, and Oprah Winfrey. Without these interesting and amazing people, this book would not have been possible.

Finally, I would like to dedicate this book to the millions of nameless, faceless black men and women in America, who continue to struggle past socioeconomic barriers which exist in our society today. It is my goal to give them a name and a face, and to contribute to highlighting our plight in this country.

"Well, if you define looting as going into someone else's turf and taking something that doesn't belong to you, you can argue that we're looting Iraq right now." – Boyce Watkins, on the Fox show, Hannity & Colmes, in response to questions about looting during the Hurricane Katrina disaster.

Preface

I sit at home alone and think a lot. A whole lot. Entirely too much, some might say. During these drawn out periods of introspective dialogue, I find myself wondering about really strange things, like whether or not Clarence Thomas really is an alien, or if some of Condoleeza Rice's friends ever come up to her and say "Giiiirl, you can't be doing foreign policy with yo hair messed up like that!" I also wonder if the musician Prince were elected President, would he then paint the White House purple and make us call him "The President formerly known as Prince"? I then wonder if I were President, would I hire someone to snuff out a person with the audacity to write a book like this about me? I probably would. Someone as annoying as myself deserves to be found in the kitchen with his face in a bowl of oatmeal.

But in all seriousness, or not so seriousness, I have really wondered and worried about our President. I love the man, I really do. It is a kind, compassionate love, the type I would have for the little puppy down the street with no hind legs. It would be really cruel to do mean things to the puppy, like take him for walks and drag him on his leash, or watch him starve to death as we tell him to fetch for Scooby Snacks.

These acts may seem cruel, but that is EXACTLY what we do to our President, as we ask him really difficult questions and force him to use words that he won't learn until the 5th grade. After hearing some of his more exhilarating quotes, I was planning to send him "Hooked on Phonics" for his birthday. But I wasn't invited to the party, which was disappointing, since I heard that they would be playing Pin the Tail on the Democrat. But move on with a broken heart, I must.

Another thing that keeps me up at night is who George Bush really is, and how I can connect with him. Not connecting in a homosexual way, but in an emotional way. I would like to understand him, so that perhaps I can understand the puppy down the street. So, through a concept we Mathematician types call "transitivity", I simply connected him to something that I understand very well, black people. I decided that it might be fun to give GW a new identity. I mean, if Michael Jackson can change his race, then so can George. The difference here is that George is getting an upgrade. Not meaning to stereotype, but he is probably going to be a better basketball player, and his hair will look a lot better than the gray and black "Crisco-boof" he wears to work every day. Perhaps he can be bald like me, with a sort of "President Michael

Jordan" appeal. He also gets to turn to Condoleeza and say things like "Talk to the hand girl!" Seeing George in his new light as a black man has enhanced my connection with him, and I can now see more clearly who he is as a person, a Republican, and as an American.

In this book, we are going to explore the parallel existence of President Bush. We are going to see who he really is, unleashing the inner-negro that lies in all of us. We are going to see what lies in store for Pookie Bush, George's fictional alter-ego as he goes through the educational system, criminal justice system, the Vietnam War, etc.

Through my journey in this book, I've realized that we seem to have a double standard. If you hate lazy people, does that mean you hate all lazy people, or just those who are lazy and poor? If you respect the president, do you respect him because he is the president or because he is a respectable person? Is a white-collar criminal treated the same as someone who steals a can of beans in a tank top?

The fact is this: If George Bush were a black man, we would probably not respect him. We would treat him the way other black men with his traits are treated: unspeakably bad and perhaps deservedly so.

This is NOT a book about George Bush (although he serves as a fascinating launch pad for the butt any jokes we might want to make). The book is about the plight of black men in America, and how this plight leads to us being expected to be modern day superheroes. Our margin of error is minimal in a society that is quick to incarcerate us, leave us unemployed, or detach us from the educational system. Many millions of men have experienced horrific fates in this country for possessing the same character flaws that might have gotten them a slap on the wrist had they been born of a different race. Have we been bamboozled? Do we think someone is someone else because of the skin they were born in or the money they have in their pocket? That is the question to ask and perhaps we can come up with our own answers.

Table of contents

If George Bush were a black man:

1) After all of his "youthful indiscretions", would his return address be Pelican Bay or Sing Sing?

Didn't he pass his third strike in the 1960s? Would a black man making the same mistakes be put IN the jail or UNDER it? My Uncle Willy was a drunk too, but we didn't even let him serve as president of our family reunion.

2) After the questionable 2000 election, who would people want to beat down more, him or OJ?

Imagine a black man accused of stealing a presidential election! Would Bill Cosby consider that to be worse than stealing pound cake? Would you be put on trial for Grand Theft Election?

3) Would Yale have admitted him instead of Clarence Thomas? Given they admit just a few more black students each year than the KKK, there is a question of whom they would consider the better token.

1

Clarence might make a far better token, since he seems more adamant in his hatred of other black people. Besides, he might have better pornos in his possession (Remember Anita's story about the pubic hairs on the Coke can? Perhaps the Coke executives watching TV that day were saying "Yes! Free advertising!")

4) He would have not only been impeached for the war in Iraq, we would have made him go over and apologize to Saddam's mother.

If you can be impeached for getting a blowjob, then I am sure you should get the same for screwing the entire country. The lies used to support this war were worse than the lies some have used on their credit applications.

5) Would he have bill collectors calling him about that trillion dollar deficit?

Maybe he could get on the "do not call" list. I just hope they don't garnish his wages. It takes a while to pay off a Trillion bucks. Maybe he could get his phone put in his baby mama's name.

6) Would he still be on welfare, as he has been for his entire life?

Daddy Bush seems to have one of the best welfare programs around. I plan to sign up myself. Isn't ANYONE who gets something for nothing technically a welfare recipient? Why do we only chastise Shaquanda with 4 kids, instead of all the students in private schools waiting for a check from their parents?

7) Would we know more about the "Super freak brother" Neil Bush than we already do?

Asian prostitutes being delivered to a married man are far more interesting than debates on public policy. I guess the media seem to have forgotten about that one.

8) Instead of hiding out during Vietnam, would he have been like one of the other hundreds of thousands of black men who actually showed up and got killed?

Even Forrest Gump knew how to follow orders. George does not. It seems easy to be a Patriot when you just pretend to have gone to war.

9) Would he have gone to an Ivy League School, or would he be in special

education like millions of other black boys in America?

I'm sure they would have pumped him up with enough Ritalin to make DMX look like a girl scout.

10) Would his black mama smack him every time he used the words "misunderestimated" and "analyzation" in public?

Ever listen to a Bush speech and find yourself thinking "Kill me please!"? If there were ever a reason to beat your kids, this would be it. If my communication skills were that bad, my mother would probably do a drive-by shooting at one of my speeches.

4

All hail Mr. President

"I know what I believe. I will continue to articulate what I believe and what I believe... I believe what I believe is right." – George W. Bush, Rome, July 22, 2001

- *Neil Bush's 1999 profit from 3 trades on Kopin Stock, $798,218 ($171,370 in one day)[i]*
- *George Bush's profits from the sale of Harken Energy stock, shortly before the share value plummeted in 1990, $848,560[ii]*
- *Martha Stewart's gain during her conviction for insider trading, $227,000[iii]*

I am probably meant to have great respect for George Bush. In fact, I do. I respect the senior Mr. Bush (President of the United States from 1988 until 1992) a great deal, as I would respect the really sharp guy who beat me at a good game of chess. I would look over at him at the end of a tough, sweaty game, and say "I hate your guts and think you're a prick, but you're an honorable and downright impressive little prick." George Bush Sr. is the perennial American hero: He's shown courage, leadership, scholarship, charisma and dedication. I even bet that his wife Barbara was a really hot babe at one point in her life. She's not quite as hot as she used to be, however, and I would even dare to say that she is downright ugly. But I am sure that she was the cutest girl at her high school graduation, even if it was back in 1871.

But this book is not about the senior Mr. Bush, it is about his son, also named George. Curious George might be a more appropriate name, but that is neither here nor there. Somehow, through a twist of really yucky fate or through some wormhole of ill-conceived logic, it was decided that little George should be the next family member to run for president. Just imagine sitting around the dinner table, in which you get to look across to one of your sons and say "Now Jeb, George gets to live in the White House first. You get to go second, but only if you eat your vegetables." That, my friends, is POWER.

To say that the junior Mr. Bush has been the black sheep of his family would be, well, an understatement. That would be like saying Bill Clinton likes women just a little bit. I am not sure how the senior Bush felt when giving his son the keys to the oval office. Perhaps he wondered, deep down, if this was the time to make an exception. After all, there had to be some other surprise birthday gift that would make little Georgie equally happy, like a rubber duckie or fake doo-doo. But his faith in his son prevailed, as he handed over our nation like an old jalopy, saying "Son, just drive right over the poor people, attack Iraq if you need gas money, and if the economic engine dies, call me or your mother." He is proud of his boy, and I don't blame him. I mean, doesn't every American parent say things to their kids like "You're going to be President of the United States one day!" In this family, such dreams become reality, while the rest of us sit to the side and watch jealously, like fat people trying to get into Baskin Robbins.

As I sat and watched the events transpire in Iraq, the economy go straight to hell, and every bit of our American livelihood be threatened out of existence, I wondered why in the world we, as a people, would choose such an unimpressive, incompetent individual to run for president. Bush is something of a real-life Forrest Gump...someone who finds himself in amazing positions in society almost by the will of God or some other supernatural force. Given that we *almost* gave him enough votes to win the election outright, I sometimes find myself concerned about our country and our choices. Have we sunk so low that we can't even appoint an *average* person to the presidency?

I have never had a problem with the fact that Bush is a Republican. I have a problem with the fact that he is a STOOPID Republican (I reserve the right to misspell that word when seeking a way to fully express the indignity of the situation). Why not choose John McCain or some other

Republican who can count to 100 without risk of aneurism? I would even take Pat Robertson or David Duke over the truly amazing Mr. Bush. Jeez, even give me Jessie Helms or Strom Thurmond. At least Strom's pro-lynching legislation would take me out of my misery. Just kidding, I don't think he would actually support the idea of lynching black women, only impregnating them.

There are moments when I hyper-analyzed my own motives for expressing such a strong amount of discontent toward Mr. Bush. "Am I jealous?" I would wonder alone in the bathtub, with the bubbles politely warming the hot funk of my armpits. Perhaps seeing him succeed with such little to work with angered me because he possessed a subtle genius that I could not access with 10 years of graduate school. Perhaps the most effective people in this world are those who can accomplish a great deal with very little effort. I've always hated these people for the ease with which they would jump hurdles that left me with my bloody forehead printed in the concrete.

But after much self-reflection, I realized that this is not the reason that Mr. Bush had me breaking out in hives. I then thought that perhaps my problems with him stemmed from the fact that he represents the snotty rich kid I always wanted to beat into the ground. As a child, I had the chance to attend (for a very short time) a very exclusive private school. It was the kind of place with tuition rates that exceeded every university in the state. So, like many schools with insanely high tuition, it wasn't worth the price. Given that the tuition level was higher than what both my parents made in a year (combined), there was no way I could have attended such a school under their financial power. So, I actually received a scholarship. I am not sure if it was a merit scholarship, for I did not have much merit to speak of. I think that it would have been better called "The Token Black Boy" scholarship, for I was the only black person...excuse me, African-American in my entire 6th and 7th grade classes. Imagine Buckwheat on The Little Rascals. That was me, in 7th grade, trying to find a way to get these white kids to like me, or at least stop making fun of my mother's car. Getting a date was not an option, since many of the students did not date those whom they believed were outside their species. So, in spite of my efforts to show the girls pictures that *proved* we were the same mammal, I was still sent to my cage at the end of the day. It could have been because I was black. It could have been because I was just ugly. I'm really not sure which one.

Attending this school really opened my eyes. First, it showed me that there were some *really freakin rich* people in this world. I mean, people with more than one car! These people didn't even have to hide every month when the landlord came by to collect the rent. They actually bought name brand stuff, like Frosted Flakes and Adidas sneakers, not the Sugar Flakes and Adios sneakers my mother would buy, making me the funniest thing in my neighborhood since Richard Pryor.

I hung out with George Bush a lot that year. He probably doesn't remember me, and given that I am about 20 years younger than him and grew up in a state other than Texas, he probably has a hard time remembering that we went to school together. Some might say that I am lying, but I say that I am just delusional. There really is a difference, since my cousin showed me that delusional people are just telling their own versions of the truth. I don't remember much about Mr. Bush from our school days, only that he stank of privilege and wore his wealth like smelly cologne. He pranced about, like a gay guy who was just asked to the prom. He made fun of me, taunted me, and reminded me that he could buy my mother with his lunch money and two phone calls. I found myself intimidated, irritated, agitated, and any other "tated" that means that I was mad. It was a rough 2 years.

So, maybe it's the presence of privilege where it appears least deserved and most exploited that yanks at my psyche. Seeing such a tragedy in the making makes you want to send God an email saying, "Come on dawg! You KNOW this ain't right!" Perhaps I was jealous because I actually had to work for things to get them, and he would get them because someone else worked for them. He can order up his daily productivity the way I order Chinese food. This is enough unfairness to make you want to smack your grandmother. And if my grandma had not taken those boxing lessons, she would be laid out on the floor right now.

Our country has had other leaders with whom I've disagreed. For the most part, I felt no need to pick at them. I was not a fan of the Reagan Era, for I recall speculating with one of my third grade classmates over how long it would take for him to have our families evicted. Also, the administration of Bush senior kept me intrigued, as I saw the words "No new taxes" seem to turn into "Bitch betta have my money."

So, as much as I couldn't figure out why, I continued to carry this nagging, persistent urge to use Bush's picture for a toilet seat cover. Then the source of my discontent finally hit me: A REALLY STUPID PRESIDENT CAN GET YOU KILLED. There was a time when I had enough faith in the nation to believe that there were plenty of checks and balances to ensure that a president did not get out of control with his power. I figured that someone would step up and say "Hey, you can't push that big red button that says 'Nuclear Warhead' just because your mom won't give you more chocolate!" But the truth is simple: a bad president might make mistakes, but a stupid president can really, really hurt you. He will lose jobs. He can cause the stock market to plummet. He can get the entire nation barbecued via nuclear war. He can cause millions to be homeless. The potential list of tragedies is longer than The Dead Sea Scrolls. Bush is not only the epitome of a bad president, but he reminds me of The Village Idiot.

The Village Idiot himself is a dangerous person under the right circumstances. Some think that he is just the guy that rides his tricycle through town with a bright red football helmet. That is far too simplistic. He is also the one that doesn't know that the hamster is choking to death as he is hugging it. He gets drunk behind the wheel and kills his own mother.

He plays with his dad's gun and shoots his best friend in the head. At worst, he tries to play God and ends up destroying his country in the process. Village idiots have squandered family fortunes, they have shaken babies to death, and they have backed the car over the family pet. *Some might say that those who put such people in positions of leadership only have themselves to blame.*

I feel incredibly sorry for the Junior Mr. Bush. Can you imagine having a dad with such impressive achievements? That's enough to make you want to sign up for a lifetime of prepaid psychotherapy. Threatened and harassed by the high standards of his family, he constantly finds himself attempting to show that he is a worthy leader, perhaps deserving of his father's withheld affection. He proves these points on our dime, as tax payer money is spent by the billions so that little Georgie can earn daddy's love. Perhaps all this could have been avoided with a 1982 visit from Dr. Phil, or even more lenient abortion laws. But now we are stuck with The White House being used as the Bush family vacation home. Maybe we should change the Pledge of Allegiance to say "One nation under Bush".

It's not as if Mr. Bush asked us to make him a leader. It is our sick, twisted fascination with his dad that somehow led us to believe that he would make a good president. He would surely have been just as happy cleaning the sidewalks or driving his dad's limo. He never would have known the difference, as long as someone rubbed his head and played the presidential theme music at his birthday party. But it was all of US who chose to make him our Commander-in-Chief. I am so frustrated that I want to go buy a gravesite so that I can start turning over in it.

When one thinks about human virtues, you can break them into two simple categories: intelligence and work ethic. When choosing a leader, stupid and hard working I can deal with. I would even settle for smart and lazy. But who ever thought it was a good idea to put a dumb, lazy person in the White House? And given that he has never officially denied allegations of cocaine use, there is also the chance that you could toss the words "addictive personality" into his set of admirable attributes. But given that the guy who made this allegation was found dead in his hotel room after "committing suicide", I should probably not bring this up. Perhaps the best way to "erase your past" is to erase someone else's future.

I am not sure I want to be a human chalkboard, at least not yet.

Given that we are choosing dumb, lazy people for the White House, I know a retarded, crack head welfare recipient who is also willing to apply for the job. Since strong credentials are clearly not a prerequisite, I am sure that you would find her urine-coated resume to be quite suitable. Oh, don't worry about the twitching, she just does that sometimes. If she starts to wobble, just give her a piece of sugar and she should be right back on track. Her twitching might make you nervous, but it's actually kind of cute, in a Condoleeza Rice sort of way. Her letters of reference are available upon request. OK, really they're not, but who's paying attention anyway?

A Trojan Horse? I Don't Think So!

"It's amazing I won. I was running against peace, prosperity, and incumbency." — *George W. Bush, June 14, 2001. Speaking to Swedish Prime Minister Goran Perrson, thinking that the cameras were not rolling.*

"'Please, don't kill me.'" – *George Bush, with his lips pursed, mocking an inmate on death row during his term as Texas Governor.*
- *Total number of executions in Texas during Bush's tenure as governor: 152[iv]*
- *A Texan who kills a white is five times more likely to get the death penalty than someone who kills an African-American.*
- *No one has <u>ever</u> been executed in Texas for killing an African-American.[v]*

Mr. Bush made things easy for us. It's not as if he were a dumb guy who looked smart. Were this the case, we could have easily convinced ourselves that his apparent incompetence was merely misunderstood genius. As I learned when studying mathematics and economics, nearly every action, no matter how silly or asinine, can usually be rationalized and justified. We can find some way to map the action back to a benevolent, thoughtful motive, or to some kind of evil, malevolent agenda. That is what American politics is all about: you basically define the person's motive to be whatever you want, depending on your incentives. If the person wants to save more trees, you say that they are anti-business. If they want to help business, you say they are anti-environment. The Ying-Yang of life

19

provides a pretty cool escape mechanism for any occasion.

Perhaps George could have made it easy for us if he were to simply make intelligent facial expressions when speaking. He could thoughtfully look into the sky every time someone asked him a question, take a deep breath and then respond with an intelligent-sounding sentence he had just heard on C-Span. As long as the words were sufficiently long and confusing, we would be satisfied that we have indeed chosen a great visionary to lead our country.

But GW has never given us this peace of mind. He doesn't look smart, for truly dumb people are not smart enough to do this. He looks confused, all the time, like a man who really can't figure out if the value meal is cheaper than getting the burger, fries and drink individually. If you really want to confuse him, add a toy to the value meal. The poor guy seems to have one working neuron, and we force him to use it every day. He presents to us a nice, stiff walk, as if he were told to walk that way. His shoulders tilted waaaaaay back like Frankenstein headed to a really important job interview. Upon seeing him enter The White House garden, I always think to myself "Frankenstein REALLY IS going to get the job this time!"

It's not as if he has hidden "himself" through his actions either. Looking at the relatively public history of George and his life is like reading "The Chronicles of Forrest Gump – on crack". He might likely represent the bad sperm that inexplicably hitch hiked its way to the egg first. Maybe that sperm took a short-cut. To this day, Professor Darwin is looking down from heaven, going "How in the hell did that happen?" Perhaps George Sr. had a little too much malt liquor on the night of conception, and ended up with something short of super-stud fertility. 9 months later, he is confronted with the living nightmare of every talented, ambitious, overachieving father: Rather than getting the great American hero you truly desire, you are "blessed" with a child that might be less than one standard deviation away from down syndrome.

Were this 100 years ago, we would not have had the pleasure of meeting George Jr. He might be tied away in his parent's attic, having bowls of oatmeal slid to him under the door. But such good old-fashioned forms of child-rearing are no longer acceptable. You've got to let all your kids out of the house: even the ones that seem half-cooked.

Some might think that Mr. Bush and I have nothing in common: He is white, I am black. His family was rich, mine was poor. I wash my hands after using the bathroom, he probably walks out licking his fingers. But that isn't true, we actually have a lot in common, and if you look carefully, the commonality transcends racial boundaries. I have several friends who have been equally reckless with their lives, one tragedy after another. One mistake after another, created by years of coddling and protection by parents who don't know how to let go. Years of living as the black sheep of the family, the one that the mother looks at and says "Maybe one day he is going to get it together." The brother in-law that you don't want calling you in the middle of the night, because you know that he is going to ask for money. The one that you won't get into the car with because you don't feel like getting shot that night.

I know Mr. Bush well, but not as the mentally-challenged, pale-skinned guy that appears on national television. I only know him in his parallel existence as a black man. He is my best friend that got shot in the middle of a drug deal. He is my drunk-ass uncle Willy. He is your cousin Pookie, the one who is not going to breath the air of a free man until the year 2054. He is the one living in his mama's basement, playing

PlayStation 2 in his underwear. He is the local crack head, the brother at the corner liquor store, your friendly Burger King shift leader. He is the waste-child of every good parent in America.

But America doesn't have the ability to connect Mr. Bush to his parallel existence. The truth of his actions are hidden by nice suits, expensive haircuts, big limos and multi-million dollar mansions. When you are a drunk, lazy frat boy at Yale University waiting for your father to send your monthly check, you are called a struggling student, not a welfare recipient. No one questions your work ethic, your value system or your desire to better yourself. You are not featured on the news as one of "those people", and you are not forced to endure the bowels of the Great American Caste System.

What is special about the dirty sock called Bush, and what dissects him away from his parallel existence as a black man is that he was born with *privilege*. Extraordinary privilege, yes, but the kind of privilege much more likely to be granted to a white man than to a black one. I would have enjoyed such privilege, for I would not have had to find out how good cereal tastes with water instead of milk. I would not know that if you hold a wire clothes hanger and stand on one leg, you can pick up more TV stations. I would not have had to watch dust flop out of my first pair of Converse sneakers donated to me by a neighbor.

When I went to college, I was a pretty well-mannered kid. I never got arrested, I never got drunk, I never got into trouble and I always kept my grades up. It was tough for me to understand why the other students could not do the same thing. It was then that I realized that many of them were protected by privilege. If they dropped out of school, they were able to go home and ACTUALLY LIVE WITH THEIR PARENTS! Rent free! Whoever heard of such a thing? I would have best friends go home to live with their moms after earning GPAs that I strongly suspect were below 0. I would hear their mothers complain about their shiftless existence for hours at a time. All the while, I'm thinking "You complain, but you do nothing. So, you must actually LIKE this." Were I to have tried to go live with my parents I would first see my mother look into the air, wondering how many years of prison she would get for killing me on the front porch. I would then have a frying pan slapped against my forehead, maybe a hot one, perhaps with some grease, depending on how many style points she wanted for this particular beating. Some call it tough love, I call it freakin child abuse. So, this

Rodney King Love, while it might have hurt for a while, actually led me to have a different value system from many of my white classmates of privilege: I knew clearly and plainly that I could not get away with the same stuff as the white kids. I knew that if I were arrested along with my white best friend, I would be the one who was selling his body to get bail money. If we both went to trial, I knew that I would be the one who had to change his first name to "7524-A". I knew that if we both squandered our money, I would be the one eating his own fingernails for lunch. That is white privilege.

It's not that every white man gets the chance to be president. Although, you could argue that becoming president is at least *possible* for a white man. Nearly every black presidential candidate has received fewer votes than MC Hammer. They always seem to get the last remaining votes thrown in the residual, after all the *real* votes are counted. I guess when a chad is hanging off the ballot at the end of the night, someone says "Hey, let's give it to the black guy! It would be like affirmative action!" In the end, the black candidate ends up looking like someone who really doesn't belong in the election, like the mascot at a football game. No one considers the mascot when choosing a quarterback. He just stands on the sideline, in his big fury Negro suit, yelling "Go Democrats!" doing back flips and push-ups every time they score a touch down.

So, as I mentioned before, it's not that every white man gets the chance to be president. It's that many white men get the chance to be corporate managers. They get the chance to receive an inheritance that doesn't involve a bill collector. They might get a new car for their 16th birthday, one that actually works. Their wedding gifts might cost *more* than $19.95.

For many, these little boosts make all the difference. I have several friends, black and white, that were one beer away from a jail cell, or one argument away from being killed in the street. Many of them were not capable or even willing to make the "right" decisions at an early age. Instead, they were just as stupid and wild as any of us were at that age. The difference is that many of my black friends suffered lifetime consequences for their youthful indiscretions, while many of my white friends were quietly shipped to the Betty Ford Clinic. Or, as much as we make fun of the young single black mother, I saw many young white girls sneaking off to Planned Parenthood to correct their little sexual mistakes. I don't condemn abortion, for I have never had a vagina under my own power (although I can always hope). But the reality is that we are all human, and we all make mistakes. The important question is why one group seems to suffer from their imperfections a bit more than the other.

Consider my friends Bob and Junebug. Seeing Bob at the age of 30, you would see no clues of the past that he once lived. He is no longer the long-haired hippie from 10 years ago. He no longer spends all his time saying things like "Where the liquor at?". He isn't jumping from vagina to vagina like the energizer bunny with a pocket full of Viagra. Instead, he was now a nice "corporate man", with a wife, 1.2 kids, a garage bigger than my mama's house, and a pretty white furry little dog that smells like Liz Taylor.

Bob might also have some quiet perks that he doesn't exactly make public, like how his bride's father paid for the wedding, shipping he, his wife, and 200 guests off to Hawaii for the ceremony. Or how his wedding gift could not be wrapped, since the store didn't have any bows large enough to cover the Mercedes *and* the roof of the new house. He also might not mention how his new father-in-law, the owner of the company, decided to boost him up the corporate ladder a little bit. After all, he was as guilty of "youthful indiscretions" as Bob was, so it is only fair that he help out the father of his grand kids. I am not sure if Bob knows exactly what he does for the company, but whatever it is that he does, he is 100% SURE that he is the Vice President of that particular thing.

So, when I see Bob for the first time in 12 years, he is living a life that makes "Life Styles of the Rich and Famous" look like the show "Good Times". Like Florida, the mother on "Good Times", I am sitting in his office going "Damn damn damn damn damn!" The office is large enough to be the Lakers' practice facility, with a nice, squishy leather chair, the kind that massages your butt crevices just right. He also has one of those annoying metal tick-tocky things on his desk. You know, the thing where the metal ball on the end moves just because the ball on the other end hit the pile of balls in the middle. The endless tick-tocks of the metal thingy create an uncomfortable silence, as Bob and I quietly ponder our diametrically opposed socioeconomic outcomes.

Of course I am impressed with Bob. And given that Bob doesn't share everything with me, I have no idea how Bob got to where he is or if/how he got any help getting there. All I know and all he knows is that his financial success CLEARLY makes him better than me. We agree on that. After all, I was still in my late 20s, waiting for a life sentence called graduate school to come to an end. Long years in graduate school really suck, and once I became a professor, I found myself saying things on TV like "I wanna give a shout out to my homies on lock-down, who got 25 to life till they do their dissertations." So, while Bob is getting the accolades that come with great financial success, I keep getting the same greeting from my relatives "So, you're stiiiiiilll in school huh?" They would then look at me pathetically and wonder if they will be going to my funeral and my graduation at the same time. I was personally betting that the funeral would come first.

During the same year I see my old buddy Bob, I see my black friend, let's call him Junebug. Many black people have a cousin or two named Junebug, so I can call him that. One of the best things about black people is that we use colorful, creative nicknames. We also don't let silly little things like logic get in the way of the names we choose. The name might make sense, it might not. It might be based on some characteristic you possess, it might not. You might know the origin of your name, you might not. To this day, people ask me if I know why I am nicknamed "Coco", and my response is the same: "I have no idea." But since everyone around me was calling me Coco, I figured that was what God called me too.

Another creative thing about black people and our nicknames is that we don't care how humiliating they are. If you eat bugars at the age of 3, then people will call you Bugar beyond the age of 43. If you become a senator, you will be the Honorable Senator Bugar. If you urinate on yourself, we will call you "Pee-pee". There are also other great names like Stinky, Pootie, Juicy, Junk-junk or Head. We don't care about your feelings. If you cared so much about your own feelings, you would not have been born with such a big forehead.

So, back to Junebug. He and Bob were once the epitome of racial harmony. I have sometimes wondered if Dr. Martin Luther King had another dream about black men and white men getting drunk together and both sleeping with the same women....in the same bed.....on the same night...*maybe* even at the same time. These guys did everything together. When one got into trouble, the other one would get cussed out by the guy's mother. Junebug was the only black kid that Bob's mother would have over for dinner, and Bob was the only white man on earth allowed to say things like "Nigga please!"

But there was a tiny difference. Bob had parents with a little money. Not a lot of money, but just enough borrowing capacity to pay a good attorney. Just enough money to pay college tuition. Just enough money for an abortion. Junebug, not having these things, but under the illusion that the world perceived he and Bob the same, found himself feeling the brunt of some of their joint "youthful indiscretions". Junebug's father probably won't be seen again before Jimmy Hoffa, and his mother, working 2.5 jobs, saw her 4 kids as much as she saw the Pope. Her hand was firm, but even the firmest hands can't handle that many kids without a working Prozac dispenser. So, some things just kinda slipped through the years, and Junebug ended up slipping through the cracks. Bob was usually his partner in crime. But Bob was not his partner in jail. Bob's mistakes just seemed to be more easily erased than Junebug's, maybe because he had a good, strong erasable pen. Junebug had no pen. He only had a Public Defender.

So, unlike my reunion with Bob, my meeting with Junebug was downright depressing. First of all, I spent a lot of years talking to Junebug through a dirty glass wall, hoping that maybe *this time* he would be out on parole. He would stare back at me wearing a bright orange, incredibly gay jump suit, and a really well-kept afro, the kind you would have if all you do is sit around patting your hair all day. He would analyze the appeal process repeatedly, with full knowledge that he would be released right after they let out Charles Manson. I would sit there and politely go "Uh-huh, uh-huh", as I wonder if he would mind if I dated his girlfriend while he was locked away. Just kidding. I had broken up with her already.

This meeting with Junebug was different, since he was finally a free man. Temporarily free, but free. Of course, the first thing that Junebug does when he sees me is borrow money. That is the universal calling card of all broke-ass people. But being equally pathetic myself, I ask to borrow money from him first, so he would know that I was broker than he was. He has a sadness in his eyes, as if his eyes had lips in them. Those lips were saying "Maaaaan, it's been a long 12 years. My life has taken me places that I don't even remember going and that I wouldn't dare even share with you. I am weary in advance for the places that my life is going to take me in the future." The sadness touches me, as I can feel the downward spiral of bad breaks, and how getting into the system at an early age essentially dooms you for life.

As much as I want to help Junebug, I have to go into protective mode. Everybody knows that the most well-intended crackhead is simply the one that feels guilty after he robs you for your money. So, with all the love and respect I have for my friend, I have to say things like "Talking to me from across the street is fine", as I wave to him from the front seat of a moving car. You end the conversation with something like "Hit me up on my cell dawg", even though you know good and well he doesn't have your cell phone number. I hate the socializing process, but "that's just the way it be sometimes".

While I was certainly afraid of Junebug, I also felt for him. I remember him when he was actually someone who didn't stink all the time. I knew when he was more likely to give an old lady a flower than to beat her over the head with sausage from her grocery bag. I had seen him in school, wanting to learn math problems that had nothing to do with kilos and grams.

Junebug and Bob had started in the same place and engaged in many of the same actions. But Junebug did not know he was coming into a ball game with a 30-point deficit. When you play with a deficit, you have to play harder. You have a smaller margin for error. You've got to play defense and offense, and you've got to be better than your opponent. Junebug didn't know this lesson. He simply thought that he could be a regular guy without being penalized for it. That is the same mistake of many young black males in America. We are not always allowed to be average.

Why This Privilege *does* Make a Difference

"Redefining the role of the United States from enablers to keep the peace to enablers to keep the peace from peacekeepers is going to be an assignment." George W. Bush, Washington, D.C. Jan. 14, 2001

> • *Number of black males enrolled in higher education in the United States in 1999: 603,000*
> • *Number of black males incarcerated in federal, state, or local prisons in the United States in 1999: 757,000 (U.S. Department of Education and U.S. Department of Justice)*

The privilege differential between Bob and Junebug matters in this world. If I were to have had the chance to warn Junebug several years ago, I would have told him that black youth are 6 times more likely than white youth to be arrested and incarcerated for the same crimes[vi]. That means that Junebug has to be 6 times as good, and has 1/6 the margin for error as his good buddy Bob. Every black parent in America seems to know this, which is why most of my black friends have heard things like "When you are black, you have to be twice as good as the white guy to get the job." Man, its hard enough just being the best, let alone *twice as good.* Does anybody ever question this stuff, or is it just me? Do they have bowling handicaps in Math and English?

The world does not judge us on where we came from or how far we've traveled. It judges us on where we finish, even if we have gone backward to get there. After my million years of graduate school finally came to an end, I had graduated from one of the top Finance programs in the world. I've concluded that this one good achievement makes up for the really stupid and evil things I've done in my life. But the glory is balanced with the fact that I get to spend the rest of my career around people who seem to think that black people should be ground up and fed to zoo animals. Seriously. I would not be surprised to wake up and find one of my less compassionate colleagues standing with a blender right next to my head.

While I've gotten some respect for the things I've accomplished, I will never be regarded as highly as an imbecile from Yale University whose dad has a million dollars in his bank account. I will never have a parent, grandparent, aunt, uncle, sibling or neighbor leave me a $200,000 home after their death. I'm just happy when they leave enough money to pay for half the funeral. People won't look at me and say "Wow. This kid started with a 17 year old single mother in the projects, and he is now a college professor." Instead, they are going to stand on their ill-conceived throne of white supremacy and ask me if I don't mind serving cheese at the next academic dinner party. Being the industrious and friendly guy I am, I say "Sure, but only for 3 hours, and as long as you pay me."

I might say that these differences piss me off. I might say that there have been days when punching my fist through someone's head would have been "oh so therapeutic". I can recall those warm, friendly days on campus during my PhD program, when I would spend class time engaged in the rather chilling, yet oddly uplifting fantasy of beating down one of my professors. During the fantasy, I would slowly walk into his office and smile as I usually did. "Oh, here comes House Negro Boyce", he would say to himself, in his friendly, yet condescending Colonel Sanders voice. But little would he know, on this day, Uncle Tom woke up on the wrong side of the bed….not the side with the "Easy-Slide Bootie Butter" that seemed to be used on all the PhD students. This was the side with the hatchet, rope and gasoline.

But I would walk into the guy's office, leaving the gas and all that stuff behind. I don't think I have it in my heart to do such a terrible thing to another person…besides, all that stuff would never get past security anyway. While this particular school was considered to have some of the greatest scholars in the world, I would argue that they actually had the most arrogant. I would hear story after story about Joey, the blonde haired, blue eyed golden boy that the professor loved so much. He would go on and on about how Joey reminded him of himself when he was younger, and how Joey was such a great fit for Harvard. Blah blah blah blah blah. At best, I would remind him of Michael Jordan. At worst, I reminded him of Dookentae Jackson, some guy with a long scratchy beard that murdered 9 people last week in a dark alley. Would he consider me a great fit for Harvard? Not unless they suddenly needed more people to pick up the trash.

So, back to my fantasy. Tom, I mean Boyce, is walking into his office with the usual "I love me some massa" smile on his face. I look at the man, he looks back. We exchange glances, and then I act: like a tiger going after a really healthy piece of red meat. I dive across his desk and pummel his ass. Do I punch him once or twice? No.

Punching someone is not worth going to jail. As my mama taught me back in the day, a good shopper gets his money's worth. *I would beat him like he stole his daddy's wallet.*

But the fantasy is not over yet. Consider this one of those Tony Soprano dream sequences. I really need the last part of the fantasy, the part where the police come and take me away. This is the part that keeps me sane. This is the part that my mother wants me to remember, for it keeps my emotions in check. Like many other members of the black middle class, I have found myself both successful and just downright angry.

So, eventually I wake up and realize that hurting people is not in my blood. That is not something that my parents raised me to do. Most of us would be Hannibal Lecter if we actually did ONE FIFTH of the things that we've thought about doing. But that doesn't mean that I wasn't pissed off. But since when did being a pissed off black man actually ever pay off? The last I checked, being pissed off and black meant being put *under* the jail cell, rather than in it.

Instead of turning the campus into my own version of "Ghetto Fantasy Island", I decided to switch schools. I chose to move to another university in the Midwest that didn't seem to think that having black students was against the law. I think that they still think that having black *professors* is illegal, so maybe they should consult Johnny Cochrane from the grave. You see? Fighting these battles even killed poor Johnny. I am sure that after hearing my pain, Johnny would then spit out one of his funny little rhymes, like "If blacks ain't here, then you don't care!" or "You don't give them PhDs, you just want them to swing from trees!" I always loved the way he turned the OJ trial into a rap concert. I personally think that he should have played background music and had some dancers in bikinis. That would have helped TV ratings.

When I finished my doctorate, there were 300 PhDs being granted that day. So, you can imagine my confusion when I was the *only* black man in the audience. Where were the rest of these men? I am not sure. I can only say that through my graduate school journey, hearing the words "You are the first black (fill in the blank)" was incredibly common. I remember thinking "Aren't we approaching the year 2000? Isn't it too late to have a first black anything?" I always thought the first black people to do something were the ones that we should see drawn in some old history book, because cameras weren't invented yet. They would be sitting there holding a broom, and maybe a shotgun, since that was the day that professors and congressmen still had to sweep the floor after work. It is flabbergasting that we were still blazing not-so-tough-to-blaze trails after the new millennium. It makes you really impressed with the gatekeepers, for after several hundred years, we've really gotten good at this racism thing. "We found out how to say nigger without using words!" I can see them saying at the Klan rally. Rather than simply protecting the bathrooms, the biggest "Whites Only" signs in our society seem to be in Academia and Corporate America. I don't care about having the right to pee next to you. I would rather have the right to get a job so that I can buy my own toilet.

At my doctoral graduation, I found myself sitting in this group of tackily dressed students. They chose

43

these really "interesting" clothe-like things for us to wear with these tilted little hats. It was a combination between Leonardo Da Vinci and Goldie the Pimp, with the clothe on the doctoral robe caressing my skin, like a sexy woman in a massage parlor.

In addition to the tackily dressed students and the snobs on stage, I recall there being two black men at the ceremony: Myself, and the former Secretary of Health, Louis Sullivan. To the school's credit, they had chosen this highly accomplished African-American as the speaker for our commencement. I was impressed, for they seemed to have forgotten that he was black. I just hope that no one was fired for the oversight.

They had supplied Louis with his own set of tacky clothing, I guess that was part of his speaking fee. If he wanted to leave the ceremony and go straight to the Playa's Ball, he could have done so without much of a problem. He looked quite distinguished on that stage, and for the first time, I looked up at someone on stage and said "Hey, maybe being like that guy wouldn't be so bad."

Of course we were going to notice each other, since the first natural instinct of any African-American is to find other African-Americans. Maybe Clarence Thomas would be the exception, since finding a white woman with giant porno-movie breasts might be high on his agenda. At least that appears to be his preference after his XXX rated circus hearing with Anita Hill in 1991. So, needless to say, Louis and I noticed one another right off the bat. I would look at him and then look away. He would look at me and then hurry up and look away. You know, the same awkwardness that all of us feel when we are looking at other people and don't want them to know it. Both of us wondering what in the hell the other was doing there, but both of us proud of the other's achievements. Both of us wanting to offer the other a ride to The Playa's Ball after the ceremony.

When I took a moment to reflect on where the other African-American males were during this ceremony, I was hit by a wave of emotion. Many of these men were probably scooped up by the very same landmines that I spent many years dodging as a graduate student. For every one black man that goes to college, there are 6 that go to prison[vii]. Maybe they were the ones who *actually did* jump over the professor's desk and beat his ass. Perhaps they were discouraged by the fact that during my many years of post-secondary education, I never saw *one single black professor* in my classroom. Talk about receiving a strong subconscious message! The message would blast into my subconscious like the guy in the cell phone commercials "Can you hear me now?" Whether I chose to read the statement or not, it was yelling at me "Hey black boy! You ain't supposed to be here! You're supposed to be on the basketball court. You're supposed to be in jail. You're supposed to be sweeping the floor, but trying to be in a place like this, you are only fooling yourself." The challenges of doctoral study leave most students wallowing in self-doubt, enough to keep you from being able to satisfy your girlfriend at night. The challenges deteriorate your manhood like wrecking balls used on the Berlin Wall. This doubt is compounded when you constantly hear that you are one of the first of your kind to attempt such a thing. These messages bang away at the subconscious of whites and blacks alike, and leave many of us believing that aspiring black doctors would be better served trying out for the NBA.

When one sees this kind of racial disparity in a certain profession, you can only come to one of two conclusions: either there is something institutionally wrong that creates obstacles for African-Americans to achieve certain positions of prominence in our society (The Pricks Blocking the Door Theory), or black people are just too damn incompetent to earn these accolades (The Black People are Still Monkeys Theory). I have many colleagues whom, perhaps because their favorite group happens to be "The Monkeys", would be quick to support the second theory. What is really scary is that these are *really smart people!* I often wonder to myself "If this is what the intellectual leaders of the free world are thinking, what do the dumb people think?"

So, if you use the standard social measuring sticks, I am not as successful as President Bush. I am not as intelligent, not as competent, not as focused. I am not as worthy and not as productive. He was meant to be great, and I was meant to be Bobby Brown. According to our society, this is true for every white man in American that makes more money than me or has a position of greater prominence. This is without regard to whether his father is a millionaire, attorney, corporate manager or politician. All that matters is where we finish, even though I was not meant to be in the race. Like that old saying goes "Some people are born on third base, and think they hit a triple."

I often feel sorry for the whites that are forced to read things like this. I am really sorry to be the bearer of painful reminders of the past, and if I had any money, I would give it to the United White Guy College Fund ("The inability to jump is a terrible thing to waste"). Just kidding, white guys dunk over me all the time. It can be tough when your privilege is thrown in your face, undermining all of the carefully nurtured illusions of grandeur that a racist society creates for you. It is like a 55-year old man dating an 18-year old super model, in which the guy truly believes that she would love him *without* the Porsche. I don't mean to take things away from people, even if it is some form of perceived supremacy. I guess it's easy to understand why someone might hate me. You know, sometimes I even hate myself. But then again, self-hatred can sometimes be the thing that holds all oppressed people together, and I am no different from anybody else.

What Would We Do With The Black Village Idiot?

"There's an old saying in Tennessee - I know it's in Texas, probably in Tennessee - that says, fool me once, shame on - shame on you. Fool me again – you can't get fooled again.", G.W. Bush quoted by the Baltimore Sun - Oct 6, 2002

- *42 percent of all African-American boys have failed a grade level at least one time by the time they reach high school..*
- *82 percent of black males between 20-21 are not enrolled in college*
- *Black males represent only 34% of black students earning a bachelors degree (The Bureau of the Census)*

Let's think about what we would do with Pookie Bush, the black version of George. The first and most obvious thing to notice about our president is that he is incredibly stupid. Lazy yes, arrogant yes, a potentially addictive and weak personality yes. But stupid is his crowning attribute, and perhaps this is what the history books will remember first. I am not trying to say that he does not have any admirable attributes, since we all have some reason to get out of bed in the morning. I am simply saying that many admirable attributes don't have real economic value, like being able to drink a beer and stand on your head at the same time.

Perhaps we can follow this intellectual exercise: assume that we could isolate Pookie Bush's lack of intellectual capability as an entity within itself. Let's go back to the age of 4. I don't want him to be a 4 year old in the 1940s, when you could actually go to school without a bulletproof vest. Instead, I would rather see him be a 4 year old in the year 2004, where he gets a chance to say hello to the prostitutes and drug dealers on his way to church. If he's lucky, they could be meeting him in the church itself. Also, let's take him out of his highly protective environment and move him into one that is not so protective, like say......South Central Los Angeles. Of course we can't give him such a successful father. That wouldn't be fair, now would it? Let's give him no father at all, how about that? That would level the playing field a bit.

The question to ask yourself is this: What would happen to this child? What if this child has no one to advocate for him, perhaps a mother who is uneducated her self? His life is an interesting one, particularly given the "lively" neighborhood in which he lives, one of those places where the bullet holes in the wall are covered with pictures of Jesus. The kind of place where hookers and drug dealers haunt every corner like Vampire chicks in the movie "Van Helsing" and the police only show up in groups of 10 and order doughnuts with their guns drawn. Where every 16 year old has gone to at least 6 funerals, and children are at risk of stepping on a hypodermic needle on their way to the sliding board.

How would Pookie Bush, the village idiot thrive in this kind of environment? Some might say that Pookie's chances of having a healthy childhood are the same as Rosie O'Donnell's chances of winning the Olympic 100 meter final. After years of ridicule, he would eventually be the nice boy that is convinced to drive the getaway car during the bank robbery, or deliver the bag of "candy" down at Big Joe's house. Survival of the fittest certainly comes into play in this scenario and he would probably not be the fittest.

Perhaps he would receive relief at school. Surely, these loving, ambitious (predominantly white) teachers from the suburbs would work with him to reach his potential so that he can overcome his intellectual deficiencies. After all, isn't that why they signed up to teach at an "inner-city" school in the first place? "Those people" need more help than anyone, so spending their time with underprivileged African-Americans gives them something to talk about at Sunday dinner. Perhaps they would love, support and nurture him like Forrest Gump's mother, who defiantly dragged her stumbling son from one doctor to another, and even screwed the school principal to help him receive a passing grade. I agree with Forrest that "Life is like a box of chawk-lettes", because "You never know which one is going to have cyanide in it".

Hopefully, Pookie's school life won't be the same as the one that I experienced during elementary school. In my 3rd grade class, to my recollection, there were two black boys: Myself, and my best friend, let's call him Joe. Joe and I were very hyper kids, extremely active. Imagine two 8 year olds after drinking 4 pots of coffee. That would be us. While we were hopeful that the teacher would appreciate the lively atmosphere we brought to the classroom, I think that she would have preferred that they lower the age of incarceration so that we could "cut out the middle man". So, I found myself seeing the principal so much that I memorized the pictures of all his kids and the colors on his bearskin carpet. I even named his fat little children: Lumpy, Hamburger, No-Neck and Butter Head. Our conversations were always cordial, like Lucille O'Ball meeting Ricki Ricardo after she had burned down the house:

"Now Boyce, it was wrong for you to….(fill in the blank)"
"But I….. (fill in the blank)"
"Now Boyce (fill in the blank)"

"But I....(fill in the blank)"
(repeat if necessary until lunch time)

I think that these conversations were practice for my arguments before a judge 10 years later, when I would surely serve as my own attorney. I am willing to bet that it would not have taken long for me to fire myself and attempt to have myself disbarred.

Through diligent effort, our teacher found ways to "manage" us. She would put us both in the back, right hand corner of the classroom, where the three of us were least likely to cross paths, or even make eye contact for that matter. Now, of course I enjoyed the corner, since that meant I could sleep, make paper airplanes or engage in all sorts of industrious activity without being disturbed by something as trivial as getting an education. I had more important things to do, like making spitballs and drawing Super Heroes. It wasn't until years later that I said "Hmm, that was odd that we were the only two black boys in the room, and we were both in the same corner of the classroom. Maybe that was why we became best friends." Perhaps this was our "Prison with training wheels". It wasn't that I had the desire to give my teacher pure hell, it was that I learned in a different way. OK, maybe giving her pure hell was a strong secondary objective. But had she embraced and understood my energy, she would have said "Hey, maybe this kid could grow up and become a smart guy that annoys people for a living." But instead, her vision was clouded by Tyrone, the guy she had seen on the six o'clock news the night before. If anyone ever looked like a baby version of Tyrone, it was surely me. As clear as day, she could see me 20 years later, with a beard and crazy, murderous eyeballs, contemplating how I was going to utilize my third strike and go out with a bang.

In my role as public speaker (a damn good one, I might add), I've had the chance to travel to a lot of school systems around the U.S. Having the sick brain of an academic, I am always seeking out meaningless patterns in the process that lies before me, just thinking about things for no reason other than the joy of thinking about them. This would be what they call "mental masturbation", from which most PhDs suffer Carpal Tunnel syndrome. I am convinced that this is why most people believe we professors have such little value to society. Personally, I believe we have great value in society: who else would single-handedly support the bow tie industry?

In my survey of the public school system, I've noticed one common, persistent pattern: Most districts are just "kinda" educating black children. I think that getting black students to graduation is pretty far down the priority list, right next to getting new bathrooms in the football stadium or buying Mickey Mouse stickers for the first grader lunch trays. In the year 2000, black dropout rates were nearly twice as high as those for white students, and black student SAT scores were 20% (201 points) lower than those of white students[viii]. The educational leadership might have very good reasons for the disparity, like black students tend to be absent from school on the day they taught reading, or black people's lips block their view of important math problems. But I would argue that the "No Child Left Behind" policy should have two extra words "...Except Yours".

Some say that the problems of the school system are the fault of the parents. Of course, we can say that parents hold some degree of responsibility for the educational outcomes of their children. But what if the parents themselves have very little education? It's not as if we are from a country that has traditionally *encouraged* African-Americans to get lots of education. So, while the educational traditions might be in Pookie Bush's family were he white, they are probably not going to be there for him as a black child. He is not likely to have a father or mother with a PhD, MD, JD, MS, DBA, MBA or any other group of letters that make you feel like you're better than other people. The reasons for this are clear, given that black people were not exactly recruited for brain surgery training in the past. Those opportunities have changed, but it might take a while before culture changes with it.

Given that Pookie's parents (well, the one that he has in the house) don't have much education, then some might say that their ability to differentiate between good education and bad education is somewhat minimized. If Pookie is going to school, well behaved and coming home with good grades on his report card, that may be all that the parent understands. It may not be until he wins that college football scholarship at the age of 18 that Pookie's mother realizes that her son can't even read his own ACT score, even though the number is less than 10.

While we can't be sure, it would not be a surprise if Little Pookie Bush were no different from the countless numbers of black children that are institutionalized at an early age. It seems at times that black children are like America's old furniture, the kind that you put into storage so that you don't have to look at it. To "help" his parents, Pookie's deficiencies would be quickly diagnosed by some smart looking counselor with tiny, wire-rimmed glasses; one who actually cares about the kids that she is destroying. As much as his mother would hate to admit it, it is made clear by all the charts, graphs and multicolored spreadsheets that her son is clearly inferior to the other children. Everybody knows that if the counselor bears the expense of printing your child's test results on colored paper, it has GOT to be serious.

To further supplement the high cost of raising such a "challenged" child, the mother might be offered what I've heard some call a "crazy check" (Supplemental Security Income): a little money every month to compensate her for the fact that her child has a learning disability. Struggling as she does, Pookie Bush's mother immediately incorporates the check into her monthly budget, buying food, diapers and school clothes with the money she has been given. If she is anything like me, her budget is addictive: Once you put something in it, you never take it out. So, even if Pookie expresses a desire to be removed from the classes for disabled students, his mother might feel the temptation to encourage him to stick it out a little while longer. After all, they *really* need the money and are *really not sure* if Pookie is ready for the regular classes. While we might want to chastise Pookie's mother for making these choices, none of us really knows how we are going to react when we've got to struggle to get our family through the week. When you're staring down the barrel of an eviction notice, Harvard University seems pretty far away.

Of course, the "crazy check" would also come with medication to mediate the deficiency, perhaps a little Ritalin to take the edge off. These drugs are good for kids like Pookie, since he can be a "quiet little moron" as they might so compassionately describe him, instead of one of those annoying loud kids that the teacher really hates. I mean, is there nothing more pleasant in a third grade class than a little imbecile who smiles politely and takes the attendance sheet to the principal's office every morning? If given the choice between a well-drugged student with intellectual deficiencies and a hyperactive Einstein, many teachers would choose the former. The Einstein would take far too long to understand and the effort necessary to nurture such a student does not draw bonus pay. Pookie is no different from many other black children in America, who are often misdiagnosed with learning disabilities[ix]. I'm sure they would pump him with enough drugs that he would think he was performing at Woodstock. Of course there is no exit strategy to get him off the drugs. That would make things too easy. Instead, the goal is to get him through the year without irritating anyone. "The rest of your life is on you dawg", I can see the counselor saying.

Finally, no psychiatric diagnosis would be complete without a set of special classes for little Pookie Bush. Like myself at that age, Pookie Bush fits the profile of students that are cut right out for special education. Between 1980 and 1990, black children were placed in special education at twice the rate of white students[x]. I guess all those psychologists are right, *black people ARE stupid.* Perhaps that is why I go to work everyday with my underwear on the outside of my pants. Or could it be the case that all human beings are actually created equally, and any test that shows one group being inferior to the other might be systematically biased?

We can't send Pookie to the classes with other children, because it is very clear to all of us that he can't do the work. In this class, we do things to accommodate the fact that these children "learn differently". In fact, we are going to assume that they cannot learn at all. What is the point in forcing little Pookie Bush to read at the age of 6, why not wait until he is 16? In fact, given that children like him have such difficulty learning, they should only go to school for half a day. There is no point in making him stay in school much longer than that, since it is torture on his little mind to make him sit still that long. Besides that, sending him home early gives us fewer kids to feed at lunchtime. There would surely be enough Sloppy Joe for everybody.

When I analyze Pookie's alter-ego, George (the guy in the White House), I step out on a limb by saying that his words don't exactly flow like Edgar Allen Poe. I then remember that unlike his spirit-brother Pookie, George was Yale educated, and probably spent his early years at some private school with lots of other rich pricks. I just wonder. What would have happened to this guy if he had gone through the public school system? I give you 5 to 1 odds that he wouldn't even be able to spell the word "USA".

The Discussion With The School Counselor

"When I'm talking about — when I'm talking about myself, and when he's talking about myself, all of us are talking about me", *George W. Bush, Hardball, MSNBC May 31, 2000*

- *Predominantly white school districts have graduation rates that are 31% higher than those that are majority minority (74.1% vs. 56.4%)(The Civil Rights Project at Harvard University – based on the percentage of 9th graders who receive a normal high school diploma in 12th grade)*

The educational perils of Pookie Bush are just beginning. The good stuff hasn't begun. It takes a lot of hard work to destroy someone's future completely, so there is a lot left to do. The system has been waiting for Pookie like the family dog at the side of the dinner table. Sitting there salivating, just waiting for the chance to throw him in the mass grave created for all black men like him.

An important day is the one in which the school counselor has a conversation with Pookie Bush. It is the same one that he has with all students in the school, in which he prophesizes as Gandolph from Lord of the Rings (also known as "The Great White Wizard") about which students are going to succeed and which should be sent to Dr. Kervorkian. No matter that some might consider it senseless to predict at the age of 12 what a child can do for the rest of their lives. The "great White Wizard" is able to see, even at this early stage, which children are destined for success, and which should be put to sleep.

He doesn't seem to consider the fact that he himself has changed a great deal since the age of 12. In fact, most of us have changed dramatically since our youth. If someone had predicted my life based upon my actions at such an early age, I would have won the "Most likely to rob whinoes for a living" award. "He be a good white man", as some of us might say about the counselor, the kind that is willing to come to the "inner-city" and work with "those kids", even though he was born and raised in the suburbs. I mean wow! He's rarely seen black people in his life, yet he has the guts to dodge bullets on his way to work and even shake their hands. We admire men like him, since he almost treats us like we're half his equal. Of course, if we were to marry his daughter, he would have us arrested, but that's beside the point.

As expected, Gandolph the counselor is going to have to learn about "these people". His disgust with their behaviors makes him take comfort in his intelligent white students that come from "good families". They don't run around with their pants hanging below their waste, listening to rap music and shooting each other in the street. They don't have 5 or 6 gold teeth in their mouths, and they actually have parents that went to college. "If only Pookie and his friends would learn more civilized behavior", he yawns to himself in his plush, wooden office.

The counselor stares down Pookie Bush, like the nasty road kill on the bottom of his front tire. Why even waste his time with this kid? It's not as if he is dealing with a future President of the United States or something. But he invests his time anyway, since spending time with Pookie is Gandolph's way of feeling good about himself when he heads back to the suburbs at night. He can ride in the Lexus his father-in-law gave him as a wedding gift and comfortably say to his hippy uncle that he has been "doing the right thing".

According to Gandolph's logic, it would only hurt Pookie to convince him that he was meant to do anything special in his life. Clearly, his hope of becoming the first black President of the United States is severely misguided. I mean, how in the world would such a great country vote a person like this into such an important position? Also, his determination to one day attend an Ivy League institution, while quite admirable, is as likely as a pig flying to the opera on a Sunday afternoon. So, in order to help this lost child, it would be important for the counselor to step in and guide Pookie toward a profession more suitable for "someone with his ability".

Pookie likes the Great White Wizard. He knows that the White Wizard cares about him as well, which is why he is spending time with him in his office today. He respects the White Wizard as he does all the other White Wizards that work in his school. He sees the White Wizard as being as great as all the white men that he sees on TV, the doctors, lawyers and accountants in the world. That is what white people do, become doctors and lawyers, so that is, by definition, what he is *not* supposed to do. If it were not for the curse of his black skin, he thinks, he would have the opportunity to reach out and do something better with his God-foresaken life. He wears his blackness like a nasty birthmark, something that was imposed upon him against his will. For he wonders that if he hates himself enough, then perhaps the others will like him. I remember feeling this way, as I thought that if I scrubbed my skin several hours each night, a beautiful white man would emerge, and I could spend the rest of my life singing Willy Nelson songs.

The advice that Pookie Bush gets, he takes. What is the point in trying to think

68

about things like college? How silly it was for him to think that he could be president. Perhaps he should pursue his dream of becoming the next Michael Jordan? He could do it, I mean he is actually the 8th tallest kid in his class. That means he is destined to be as tall as Shaquille O'neal. He doesn't dance or sing very well, so there aren't many other job openings for black people for which he is qualified.

As time goes on, going to school is getting more and more difficult for little Pookie Bush. He is ostracized by his teachers, and placed in the back right corner of the classroom with Boyce, the other mentally challenged kid that likes to misbehave, and both of these little jerks are positioned to produce as little disruption as possible. We don't mind, we just sit back "kickin it" until the bell rings and it's time to go home. That is how Pookie and I become the best of friends.

Pookie Bush Discovers The World of Drugs

"Laura and I don't realize how bright our children is sometimes until we get an objective analysis." George W. Bush, Quoted in The Bush Dyslexicon by Mark Crispin Miller W. W. Norton, 2001

- *Between 1980 and 1994, for every 1*
  black male that was placed in the higher
  education system, there were 6 added to
  the prison system (National Center for
  Education Statistics, Bureau of Justice
  Statistics)

George Bush's alleged substance abuse history[xi] is about as storied as the Canterbury Tales. It almost seems that his only memories of the 1970s and 80s consist of two things: lighting up and waking up. When asked if he's ever used cocaine in the past, Bush has been as evasive as a dude with 10 baby-mamas. In politics, a non-denial can be as bad as admitting something. When every other presidential candidate flat-out says that they've never used cocaine, it's awfully funny when you're the one guy who didn't catch the question.

I've had friends who've spent several years of their lives involved with drugs. The difference is that they also spent the bulk of their mid life crisis using phrases like "Phone check nuggah!", as they fight with the other guy in their cell block who is keeping them from calling their girlfriend.

But let's do the Michael Jackson transformation once again and turn Mr. Bush back into a black kid. He is Pookie again and in this parallel universe, he and his destiny date with drugs occur about the age of 16. I may be adding a few years, since Mr. Bush may have started using drugs much earlier. I am convinced that it takes a lifetime head start to become confused enough to choke on pretzels during football games.

Given the grim diagnosis from his counselor and the fact that there really isn't much to live for anyway, Pookie Bush, like many youths with nothing to live for, eventually turns to drugs. Drugs are a nice way to ease the pain and to be hip. They are also cheaper than psychotherapy. Getting drugs in the hood is as easy as getting a cowboy hat in Walmart, so it's not uncommon for Pookie to have a little weed, and perhaps even a little crack. A wealthy white man might turn to cocaine, but crack really has a nice "punch" to it, and who can really afford cocaine anyway? Of course, Pookie is too young to understand that he would be better off with cocaine instead of crack. U.S. mandatory drug sentences dictate that when his black butt is caught with crack cocaine, he is going to end up with a prison sentence so long that his casket will have stripes and a cellmate. Doesn't he know that U.S. mandatory drug sentences gives prison terms that are 100 times longer for those who possess crack instead of powder cocaine? [xii] Someone might also want to tell him that even though whites are 5 times more likely to use illegal drugs, blacks make up 62% of all drug offenders in state prisons.

As expected, Pookie's casual drug use eventually gets out of control. He even sells drugs to make money. What other options are there? The White Wizard told him that education is not quite up his alley, and since he wants to "bling bling" like all the other kids on the block, selling drugs seems to be the easiest way to get there. Sure, there are people who die every other month, and sure some guys go to jail every now and then, but that just means that they are "keeping it real". At the same time, he, like every other mammal on this earth, has ambition. He wants status, for all men know that status is the only thing that opens the path to the obtainment of a vagina of your very own. Without money, power and nice possessions, his only sex life will consist of plastic blow-up dolls and his own late-night renditions of "Jack the Ripper".

If you want to understand men and their ambitions, all you have to do is watch The Nature Channel. This is Mother Nature at her best, showing the most primitive instincts that all mammals possess, and how deep down, we are all pretty screwed up. Watching whales, lions, and bears deal with one another is how you can truly see what lies in the depths of all of our hearts. They don't care about what is politically correct or socially acceptable. They are pure instinct baby, pure instinct. On this show, if your woman wants another guy, you flat out kill him. You don't take him to court, and you don't go to therapy. You just chew on his neck until he drowns in his own blood. If you are an animal dude, you are a *real* dude. You don't just have one wife that asks you take out the trash and fix the satellite cable on the roof. You get an entire harem of female lionesses waiting for you to come home and impregnate them all. The females on The Nature Channel keep track of which males are the strongest and which are the weakest. They don't want to mate with the wuss: the little scrawny guy that the other antelopes beat down every night. They want the big powerful antelope. The one with massive testicles and a big sheep's carcass on his living room floor. That is the one that gets to make all the babies. Sorry buddy, that's just the way it is

So, we sometimes wonder what drives us as people. We wonder, as guys, why we have this urge to castrate the guy who took our girlfriend. We wonder why we put so much effort into bling-blinging and attempting to obtain power. We wonder why one girlfriend is not enough for a lot of men. You want to know why? Just watch The Nature Channel.

Pookie is no different from his mammal counterparts. He too wants power. He wants status. He wants to bling-bling. No one understands this better than his homeboys, who supply him with many "possiblingities" in the hood, like selling things, carrying things and doing things that are going to lead to financial prosperity. In this regard, he is no different from his alter-ego George, but with a change in venue. He is ambitious like an old prospector out west in the 1800s, just trying to "get hiz" like everybody else. In many circumstances, we might admire this ambition, for he is a man with courage to pursue his dreams, at times with great possible cost. We admire men that run off to Iraq to shoot Arabs in the head, or those who killed the Nazis in World War II. But Pookie is not admired for his desire to follow his instincts, he is expectedly vilified and asked why he couldn't just work at McDonald's like all the other uneducated guys in the hood. When a man has no educational options, then fast food or illegal activity are his only choices. Many of the more ambitious types are going to choose the illegal route, but wouldn't that make them similar to the outlaws who fought for independence in the American Revolution? After all, the patriots were also people who had no choice but to illegally violate the system that had given them no other options.

When Pookie is finally caught selling drugs (and he WILL get caught), he gets to find out first hand how the legal system works for a young black man with no money. This is not the legal system that the founding fathers put in place, but rather, the other one designed by Adolph Hitler. The word for the day is not "rehabilition". A better word might be "extermination". One could almost hear the prison warden saying, in some dark creepy voice "Hey little booooy. I've been waiting for yoooooou!"

Pookie's white alter-ego George, could simply call his dad's lawyer, who would rush to make bail and get him out of jail. But this doesn't work for Pookie Bush, who is forced to pass his time behind bars, waiting for his court date. Yeah, it's a little stinky, but he has seen worse. His attorney is not the highly paid, Harvard educated lawyer he wishes would come to his rescue. Instead, it's some alcoholic, over worked public defender, with a pile of files on his desk the size of Dallas Cowboy Stadium. His goal is not to seek justice. Any good American citizen knows that real justice costs money. If you had really wanted justice, then you would not have the audacity to have been born so damn poor.

When he meets with Pookie, the attorney doesn't sit him in a plush office behind an oak desk, carefully describing his options. He meets him in a cold cell with a metal table in the middle and describes to this guy in an orange jump suit how he had better plead guilty or expect to spend the rest of his natural life behind bars. There are two options: either a million years in prison, or a million years with parole after he is dead. The decision needs to be made quickly, since lunch is in 30 minutes. The options are presented with the added threat that fighting the charges, even for an innocent man, is going to bankrupt his mama, who has mortgaged the house to pay for his defense.

Pookie can try to explain that this is his first offense. He can explain that he wants to do something better with his life. He can even argue that he is innocent of the charges. Such argument would fall on ears that only hear the cha-ching of dollar bills. In America, justice is sold in the grocery store, right next to liberty, in the Protection and Freedom Isle. An African-American might be able to walk through the door, but food stamps don't buy a thing in The Grocery Store of Justice.

Years later, Pookie is finally released from jail. What about the rehabilitation that he was promised? The state prison system has about as much rehabilitative capacity as a crack house. The Martha Stewart version of incarceration, Federal Prison, can be more like a country club than anything else. It also does a nice job of making sure that the rich guys don't have to find boyfriends to protect them in the night. I was thinking about vacationing there next summer. State prison, where Pookie is going, is dark and gloomy, like some kind of really scary Batman film. The guards seem as big as monsters and as lively as zombies, as they stand in their towers with guns pointed at your earlobes while you shoot basketball. I've visited state prison many times to see friends, and the sight of the building makes me want to kill myself in the parking lot. What is really sad is that I have seen urban middle schools that look the same way. You would hope that Pookie would have a chance, but not as a young black man. While African-Americans comprise 13% of all drug users, they make up over half of all drug convictions[xiii]. So, sorry Pookie, the odds are stacked against you buddy. It appears that he loses again on the "Negro wheel of Fortune".

When Pookie emerges from the prison walls, he is no longer the energetic 18-year old he was when originally incarcerated. Rehabilitation is about the 94th priority of the criminal justice system, so it is much more likely that he is a meaner, more disgusting person now than he was when he was 18. He no longer possesses the naiveté he took with him behind the prison walls. That special innocence was robbed of him on a cold night during his first weekend in "the joint" and replaced by the injection of a virus with four big letters that will plague him for the rest of his life. He takes medication for the virus along with his Ritalin, which has allowed him to live for as long as he has. He will even take the liberty of sharing the virus with many nameless, faceless women waiting to cheerfully greet him outside the prison walls.

Getting a job after leaving prison would certainly be a viable option were Pookie, say, a former Enron executive. If he were Kenneth Lay, there would surely be many foundations waiting to hire him for his consulting experience. He would not be the hottest commodity, but if he were a well-dressed white man from Yale, perhaps his father could "make a few phone calls".

No such luck for Pookie Bush. Being black is bad enough, but being a black man with a prison record makes him about as employable as Spuds McKenzie. He may as well have kept himself in prison, since that is the land that he knows so well.

I have seen people like that. Those who don't really get out of prison, they just "come visit". Celebrities have their "15 minutes of fame" and these guys have their "15 minutes of freedom". Any plans made with this person more than a week in advance are scheduled the same as the NBA Finals - "To be played if necessary". This is the kind of guy that carries his prison habits and memories with him. Maybe he is still wearing his clothes from 1985, and eating steak with a spoon, since he is not used to sharp objects. Too many men have been forced to adapt to prison life, and I find it ironic that no one really discusses the fact that black men are being incarcerated at such a high rate. Do we think that this is going to *help* society? Are they like an army of roaches that society is going to just sweep under the rug? Believe me, I tried sweeping roaches under the rug when I was a kid, and it never worked. I would always end up with something prickly crawling across my nose in the middle of the night.

Why Mo Money is Better Than No Money

"They misunderestimated the fact that we love a neighbor in need. They misunderestimated the compassion of our country. I think they misunderestimated the will and determination of the Commander-in-Chief, too", George W. Bush, Washington, D.C. Sept 26, 2001

- *Proportion of white households which possess 0 or negative net financial assets: 25.3%*
- *Proportion of black households which possess 0 or negative net financial assets: 60.9%*[xiv]

On the cold, lonely nights that I usually spend in front of my computer, working on some research problem that has me one cuss word away from an aneurism, I have often wondered to myself: what would it be like to have an uncle leave me $100,000 in cash? What about having a parent leave me a house worth $300,000? When I finished school, I had so much student loan debt that I was legally forbidden to say the phrase "IOU" in public. If Debtors Prisons were still in existence, I would have gotten the electric chair. The idea of starting off at the age of 22 with a positive net worth is about as foreign to me as marrying a Chinese Chicken. Having more debt than the Federal Government is not new in my family, since I am actually doing *better* financially than many of my relatives. So, in spite of the fact that things could be better in other states of the world, I don't complain. I might observe, analyze, mention, discuss, bitch, kick, scream, moan and whine, but I don't complain. Remember: being a pissed off black man in

America only increases the chances that you are going to be on the six o'clock news. For many members of the "angry black middle class", bedside Valium would seem to be the drug of choice.

I have always known how to work hard, and it's always been my assumption that because of my background and ethnicity, I am going to have to work harder than the white boy across the table. I remember years ago, my parents telling me things like "You are always going to have to work twice as hard as white people to get half as much." They would also say "Don't think you can act like the white kids and not get into more trouble than they do. Their parents can bail them out, and the police are going to give them breaks that your black ass won't get". Talk about making you feel like half a person. I would guess that someone who has to do twice as much to get half as much is being told that he is about ¼ as human as the person he is being compared with. When you are a black man, there is no such thing as a routine traffic stop. All traffic stops mean putting your hands on the wheel and not moving your eyeballs too much, for you might be picking bullets out of your teeth.

But there are also the days when I say "Why do I accept the fact that I have to do twice as much as everyone else? I mean, is that the way it is *supposed* to be?" When you're walking 5 miles to get to the store, and everyone else is zipping past you in sports cars, you are going to eventually get a little irritated. The only question at that point is "Do you car jack someone, or do you just keep walking until you can save enough for your own car?" The verdict is still out on me, but I do know that the blisters on my feet get a little bigger every day.

What about Pookie Bush? If he were the son of a rich and powerful politician, he would surely have been given access and opportunity far beyond his capability. He would have had the chance to run corporations into the ground, and make millions in consulting fees doing damn near nothing. He would have gotten chance after chance after chance, even if he were an absolute screw up far beyond the age of 40. When one analyzes the life of his white counterpart, Curious George, we see that he has had chances that most of us will never get. I found his Insider Trading allegation with Harken Energy to be especially interesting. I would consider $848,560 to be a nice day's work, especially in 1990 dollars. Heck, even in 2050 dollars, it would be more than lunch money. As a Finance Professor, I was especially floored and found it quite ironic that the company tanked right after Bush chose to sell his stock. That is what we in the Finance profession might call a "pump and dump", where the inside guys take the outside normal people (aka. You and me) and hand us our asses in a coonskin cap – just think Enron. Basically, if he sells the stock and makes a ton, then someone else has bought the stock and lost a ton. What is awfully ironic to me is that we're talking about NEARLY A MILLION BUCKS! I mean, if Pookie can go to jail till the year 3000 for doing $50 worth of drug business, shouldn't a guy at least get a little time for jacking you for a million bucks? Heck, I would even agree to do a year in prison if you let me jack somebody for a million bucks before I go. At least my limo would be waiting for me when I got out. Technically, Curious George was not caught stealing, since the SEC declined to investigate his insider-trading allegation. How convenient that must be, since this particular case had more red flags than a Chinese province.

Even beyond money, were Pookie born of privilege like his brother George, he would find that having a powerful parent leads to other types of inheritance. He would be more likely than his minority counterparts to have a father, uncle, aunt, brother or cousin that works for a wealthy law firm. He would have those connections in the event that he decides to sell expensive vacuum cleaners and needs clients that can pay $2,000 to clean their floors. This would be different from living in the projects, where your potential clients are all trying to borrow money from you.

I can remember when I got my first high paying job. I think that some of my relatives thought I should change my name to The First Bank of Boyce. Fortunately, I have siblings and parents that are strongly self-sufficient. They make fun of deadbeats like I do. I do have some cousins and friends that suck the life out of you like leaches with diarrhea. It's not that the draining makes you angry, it's just that when you are black in this country, all the poverty makes you more likely to be a drainee than a drainer. Those who find themselves able to get ahead and make a little cash are quickly bombarded with lots of requests for loans to solve "temporary" financial problems. But later you find that the only thing temporary about the loan is that the person's memory becomes too short to remember that they borrowed money from you in the first place. There are days when I long to be able to drain others the way that others have drained me. I want to be able to call people in the middle of the night and say "I am going to need another 5 grand cause I lost the first 5 thousand you sent me. I think it's in the kitchen somewhere." Instead, I usually receive the phone calls, and I pretty much consider all loans to be donations, since you are not going to get the money back. Also, the money is a great tool to get rid of people that you don't want bothering you anyway. Once they get the money, they quickly become milk carton kids.

I once knew someone who was in the same predicament. He and I both were in our early 30s, earning six figure salaries. So, some would say that we had it good, and I guess it shows that going to school for 120 years in a row can be a good thing. Our bond was partly due to the fact that we had endured our years of torture as graduate students, and I was now a young faculty member, with a life full of butt-kissing and butt-greasing. There were days when I flat out hated my job, since being one of the first black men in your profession is a lot like being the first man on Mars. The only difference is that on Mars, you are less isolated, and more likely to make friends. I admit that I did a little less butt-greasing than some of my other black colleagues, many of whom would have made great fairy tales of "The good negro", the one that massa always loved. Some of these guys had cow-towed their way into elite institutions. I would go to conferences and see one guy in particular, someone that I dislike more than sauerkraut sandwiches. Of course, he was always quick to show me how he was better than me, which I pretty much quietly accepted and ignored. Like the House Negro with the pretty white suit, he would stand over me as I wore my dirty overalls, ready to go back into the field. "Boyce, you're so bright and talented", he would say. "If you would just plaaaay the gaaaaaame and make the white faculty members like you more. You would be so much more successful, just like me." He would look at me sympathetically, like a koala bear that has no idea he was about to be put in the gas chamber. I would look back at him curiously, as if I am wondering if he actually gets money after letting his boss have sex with him.

Going to academic Finance conferences is a funny thing. Like the best British bloodhounds, people are keenly aware of two things about you: Who you are and for what university you work. Meeting a new colleague means that you have to go through their subconscious "registration process". The person would not look you in the eye. He would scope down at your nametag like you've got two big double D breasts with a yard's worth of cleavage. He (and it is usually a "he") would then categorize you: either you are "better" than him, meaning that he was determined to spend the entire interaction with his nostrils up your ass, or he was "better" than you, meaning that he was therefore entitled to ignore you. So, depending on how you looked at it, my affiliation with Syracuse University either drew instant toe massages, or the white man's version of "Talk to the hand".

Being one of a small number of black people at these conferences made them even more fun. I always hoped that the conference would be held in an urban area, that way I could make friends with the people serving food. Every now and then, I would actually talk to my colleagues, including the prick I mentioned earlier. Even though he and I knew one another, I would not get eye contact. I would get the "I am listening to you, but I am looking past you to see if I see someone more important" look. I didn't mind the look, since that is just what pricks do. Also, what fun is it to be a good House Negro if you can't make fun of those whom you do not consider to be as successful as yourself? So, I understood his need to make me feel inferior to him, for that is the only way that he could feel truly superior to me.

The other friend I mentioned (the good one) would often spend time with me at these conferences. We had a lot in common, since we were both from humble beginnings, unlike the wine and cheese eating, bow-tie wearing clowns that fill our profession. He was from the Deep South. The part of the South where Juneteenth is not the celebration of blacks being freed, it's the advance celebration of the day that they might actually be allowed out of slavery. He would tell me about the adventures his relatives would put him through. Man they were humdingers! I'm talking about parents calling to ask for money just because they heard that you made a deposit into your bank account, or hearing about your brother's pending eviction only after he has not paid his mortgage for six months. Add that to the realities of six figure school loans, and you get the point. We didn't complain about our plight, since it was better than most, but the fact was that we were getting drained. He and I once wondered aloud "We help everyone else, but if we ever needed some help, no one would be there." So, we're like the firemen who wonder, "What would happen if the station were burning down?"

Some of these issues relate to Pookie Bush. If Pookie were white, his inheritances and rites of passage would not be draining, they would be supportive and uplifting. The family net worth differentials between black and white families is over $46,000[xv], so just being white by itself is like being a baby with a booster chair. He would find that Police are actually there to protect him, not to scrape his brains out of the front seat. He would find that getting the manager of IBM to consider him for a second interview is a lot easier, since they both have blond hair.

Money matters. Someone with the less than desirable personality traits of a Pookie Bush, with no money to boot, has as much of a chance of making it in this world as a ham sandwich has of getting through a fat farm. He is going to live and die with nothing but debt, and the only way he could get $10,000 from a relative were if he were to rob his relative's boss. So, anything that this man gets in the world, he is going to have to earn from scratch. That is the reality he lives with as a black man in America. Sure, there are avenues to success, but it is a little tougher to sprint in a mud puddle when you started 100 yards behind the other runners. As a black man, his mud puddle is his community, which continues to suffer, even when he is successful. He cannot turn his back on his community, for if he is the least bit successful, there are those who are going to rightfully remind him that he stood on the backs of others to achieve his success. So, even if he were to become a doctor, lawyer or Indian Chief, he would still have the same problems as the average black man. Not that I am complaining, but then again, I probably am. So, I work hard, I complain. I get results, I complain. I move forward, I complain. What good is it to overcome all this crap if you don't get in somebody's face and yell about it?

The Right to be Lazy

"Why don't you mentor a child how to read?" George W. Bush, St. Louis, Missouri Jan. 5, 2004

- *In 2001, the high school graduation rate for African-Americans was 51%. That for African-American males was 43%. In fact, the method of calculation provides misleadingly high results, so the numbers are actually lower (The Civil Rights Project at Harvard University, based upon the percentage of 9th graders who go on to earn a normal high school diploma)*

One thing that is interesting about the world is that hard work can carry you a long way. But it can never carry you as far as you will go if everything is handed to you. One thing I found to be remarkably impressive about George W. Bush is his ability to go so far with such little effort. I have rarely seen anyone work so hard to ruin his life, yet still end up with the greatest job in the country. Only in America!

Lazy people have a place in the world. It's not quite in the Oval Office, but there are other things they can do, like sit at home and wait for the welfare check to arrive. That welfare check may be coming from the government, or it may be coming from the rich daddy who thinks that his kids need financial support until the age of 30. I know a few guys who live under their mother's roofs past the age of 30, and they are never rewarded or respected for such impressive shiftlessness.

What I find quite interesting, however, is that someone like Paris Hilton, the dirty little rich girl in New York, is never ridiculed in the same way she would be if she were a young black mother on welfare. I don't agree with either lifestyle, but I find it ironic that it is only the poor black person that is "dissed" for being lazy. Don't black people have the same right to be lazy as white people do? Or is hard work only an attribute that minorities are forced to embrace? Perhaps they should create a new constitutional right: The Right to be a Lazy Ass. If I were a Senator, I would propose that bill tomorrow. Not that we would *encourage* people to be lazy asses, we would just give them the right to do so if they felt so inclined. Sort of like pleading the 5th, or going into protective custody: it's not that we *want* you to do this, but you can do it if you choose.

Such a right would be as important as the right to work. While most of us know that being lazy is not going to get you anywhere, we are fully aware that some people can be lazy and never "called out" for their behavior. I am not here to say that GW is lazy. I can only say that it's hard for me to imagine a hard worker who spends lots of time going AWOL from his job, or who admits that he was on continuous drinking binges. It's also hard for me to imagine such a hard working person being ostracized by his parents for being a complete bum. We've all been lazy-asses at some point in our lives. I can think of many afternoons in which I've sat on the couch and done my best imitation of the Greek God, "Fatbuttickus". I would sit until algae started to grow in my behind, then I would take a shower and begin the process all over again. The only thing that makes us all different is the penalty that we pay for our own inadequacies. As a black man, my penalty for laziness would be a life sentence of poverty and misery. George Bush's penalty is that he had to wait until he was over 50 to become president.

Due to their position in society, a lazy white kid has a greater likelihood of being forgiven for a lack of ambition occurring as a result of youth. He is more likely to be allowed to spend the first 20, 30 and sometimes even 40 years of his life growing up and learning to be mature and responsible. Not that this is true for all white kids of course, but it is statistically true, due to the fact that being white means that you are several times more likely to be born with a middle class income. And given that Dr. Spock has come along and forbade all parents to beat their kids (many black mamas have never read Dr. Spock, at least not my mother), some of these kids get away with murder, sometimes figuratively, sometimes literally. If I were to have tried some of the antics of my friends, it would be *my mother* getting away with murder, as I would feel the broomstick go into my eye.

As a black child, Pookie Bush is not allowed the luxury of sustained incompetence. Academic laziness (which was probably part of my problem as a child) is usually misdiagnosed at a very early age as some kind of learning disability, and if the child is put on serious medication and into the wrong classes, then you may as well put up a sign that states "GAME OVER". When a child isn't educated early, they are probably never going to be educated. By the time the child wakes up and realizes that he has been had, it's far too late.

Pookie Bush, being the lazy black kid he is, certainly doesn't get to go to college. He doesn't get to be the CEO of a corporation, and he doesn't get to go into politics. If he were even a regular white kid, he would, on average, have the chance to at least do SOMETHING that supports his family. He would not have to deal with the misery that awaits any black man who is not used to working his butt off to get ahead.

Having the wrong values would destroy any chance Pookie might have of becoming somebody in this world.

My resentment of the higher burden placed on African-Americans is driven by the fact that as a statistician, I know that it is *impossible* for an entire population of people to be above average. By definition, the word "average" means that half are above that point, and about half are below. If everyone were above the average, then that number could no longer be the average. Sort of like having 5 people on one side of a see saw, it just doesn't work!

Oftentimes, I will hear other African-Americans place a greater burden of the plight of blacks onto black people themselves. Some might say "We would be even with the whites if we would just stop spending our money on gold chains and new cars.", or "We could get ahead if we would just stop being so darn lazy all the time." Granted. Having a nation of 33 million Super Negroes would certainly solve the problem. But let's be clear: not every person is going to be the "Six Million Dollar Bionic Black Person", nor should they be forced to become that person. Why is it *not* my right to spend money on a gold chain if I want one? Why is it *not* my right to buy a new car? Are you saying that whites are ahead financially because they don't buy cars or gold chains? No. While it is clear that the status of black folks in this country is going to take a lot of hard work to overcome, we must understand that this problem was created by *many of us working together, not just the black people.*

This reminds me of a friend that was molested by her father for many years. In fact, her father was having sex with her as far back as she could remember. Through years of living with a sexual predator, this young woman, being the tough survivor that she was, was forced to use some very difficult and sometimes unhealthy coping mechanisms just to get through the day. She didn't know the mechanisms were unhealthy, she just knew that they were critical to her very survival.

As you can imagine, years later, many of those mechanisms were still in existence. She would sometimes do things that the rest of us might find sad and at times, morally problematic. Were we to see this child at the age of 28, we would say to her "Look, your dad is gone. It's over. Grow up and start acting normal!" And while she is partially responsible for her behaviors, the reality is that she has become addicted to a way of thinking that was the result of years of undeserved abuse in her household.

According to American courts, her father would not only suffer severe legal penalties, he would also be forced to pay a great deal of money in a civil judgment. The *last* person we would blame for the abuse would be the victim.

At the same time, the victim herself would face the burden of working to adjust her own actions from that day forward. This might be achieved through many years of therapy, and we would expect the process to be a long, slow one. It took a long time to create the problem, so it is probably going to take a long time to fix it. In fact, it takes longer to build something up than it does to destroy it.

Black America is the abused young woman. But the difference is that she still lives with her father, and in his shame, he does what he can to forget what has happened. In fact, some would say that he is still sneaking into her room in the middle of the night. But now that she is much older, she can fight off his advances. He doesn't want to discuss the events of the past over the dinner table, he would instead rather not talk about that issue. After all, he has agreed to pay for her to go to college and he gives her a healthy allowance. Some might call this hush money, some might call it guilt money. Who cares? It's money, right?

With all the donations African-American organizations such as the NAACP and the Urban League receive, it's very easy to see that this guilt/hush money serves as a nice "calming factor" for the movement toward true reparations. But the abusive father is not interested in giving his daughter reparations, for they would ruin him financially. After all, he is a better man, so he feels that there is no reason he should suffer for things that happened in the past. All the while, the child still suffers from the pain of the past, and the everlasting impact that the past has on the present. Sort of like having your arm amputated, and then being chastised because you can't dribble to the basket with your left hand.

Interesting Elections and Loyal Baby Brothers

*"The legislature's job is to write law. It's the executive branch's job to interpret law.",
George W. Bush, Austin, TX, November 22, 2000*

- *Number of predicted votes for Pat Buchanan in Palm Beach County: 630 (where alleged voting "problems" took place in Florida)*
- *Number of votes Buchanan actually received: 3,407[xvi]*

Like the rest of the nation, I watched the 2000 presidential election with my jaw scraping the concrete. I mean, I can certainly appreciate the value of most subtle forms of government corruption, since that is what makes the world go round. Heck, if I were president and my brother were governor of Florida, both myself and my mother would make a 3-way phone call to him, saying "You ARE going to make sure that your brother gets the election, aren't you?" Any refusal by my brother would be met with the age-old threat "Just wait till your father gets home." The election in the Watkins family would surely be a family thing "Us against the world". We would boldly extort one another into massive guilt trips, as we quietly deleted the votes of all those in our state who don't really deserve the right to vote anyway. I mean, do they *really* know what to do with those important votes? If they are not Yale graduates, then probably not.

What is really interesting about the election is the bias in the manner by which the actions of the election were interpreted. Exactly how much circumstantial evidence is required before it is as valuable as concrete proof? What if Pookie, in all his ambition, does somehow get the chance to fix a presidential election? Let's assume that Pookie's brother, "Rerun", is the Governor of Florida. Pookie knows that if white people are allowed to vote, it's going to destroy the chance of him winning in his brother's state. But even after months of politicking and lining pockets of certain white leaders, he is still unable to hand his brother the election. That is when we go to plan B.

Rerun, in all his loyalty, makes sure that any white man that shows up at the poles has his background checked for outstanding parking tickets or arrest warrants. Maybe he sets up a Starbucks next to the polls to distract them on their way to vote. He also lets them know well in advance that if they show up, the background checks are going to occur, so showing up to the poles is going to be a risky proposition. He also makes sure that the list of felons is expanded and backdated in such a way that as few whites as possible are allowed to vote. To make things even more interesting, Rerun seems to "overlook" chaos in the voting system that will ensure that the votes from certain districts are not counted.

What is the outcome? Rerun hands Pookie Bush the election. In spite of all the protest, Pookie's pathetic butt is the next president of the United States. So, there Pookie stands, gold teeth and all, basking in his glory as President of the United States. He brings his "Presidential hoes" (as he calls them) in by the limo load, to ensure that he gets a good return on his newfound prestige. I mean, as Bill Clinton showed us, what good is it to be powerful if you don't get to use that power to obtain extra sex? If you don't think power matters, go back to The Nature Channel. For nearly every mammal on the face of the earth, the strongest male always gets the most women. So, Bill was not really the big freak we want him to be, he was simply embracing his human nature......uh, ok.

Surely, the country would not stand for Pookie's black butt getting away with such a crime. The audacity of two black men to swindle the entire country out of their right to vote is simply unacceptable. The protest would ring in "O.J.esque" proportions, as the nation would scream at the top of its lungs from sea to shining sea. The OJ trial showed us that when black men use the system to cheat the system, people throw tantrums. If these same events were to occur in a third world country, the reaction would be the same. Think about it, a man wins a highly questionable election by allegedly stealing votes in the state *governed by his brother!* That's serious Jerry Springer stuff. Perhaps the media can help by bringing up Pookie's checkered past in their news stories? Maybe we can talk about his daughters and their drunken nights at the club? Maybe we can discuss his brother Neil and his wild nights with Asian prostitutes? Whatever it takes to get this immoral guy out of office, we are willing to do it.

Pookie wouldn't even be in the Oval Office long enough to replace Lincoln's picture with the one of the Black Jesus. There would be congressional hearings, trials and all kinds of other complicated crap that would surely destroy the political career of this horrible man. We would even bring up his drug use from the past and any questionable associations he might possess. Destroying his political career would be a matter of national security. He would be considered a dictator, an Adolph Hitler kind of man.

But for some reason, little of this occurred when George Bush ran for the

White House. Don't get me wrong, there were lots and lots of questions. But the scathing political windfall that would have occurred if he were black did not take place. Of course, some of this has to do with coming from a powerful family and having the support of the Republican Party, but I think that even if the candidate were Colin Powell, all the doo-doo would surely have hit the fan.

Such is the experience of powerful black men in the media. Eventually, any good image is going to be destroyed. The only images that are supported tend to be those that fit certain stereotypes. Notice that even the great Denzel Washington was not recognized for his tremendous acting ability until he did the movie "Training Day", in which he played a dirty cop with no morality to speak of. I would wonder to myself, usually out loud as I screamed at the TV "What! Is that the image you have of black people?" I would wonder to myself why Denzel, who has been acting for many years, was not recognized for his great roles in Malcolm X, or even Crimson Tide. Had he improved *that much* as an actor since playing John Q? Was it the *actor* or was it the *part* that won the award? Was he finally being rewarded for playing a "realistic" black character? After all the "interesting" images of African-Americans in the media, did we *really* need everyone going to see this particular Denzel Washington movie?

Also, during the "Negro night at the Oscars", the Best Actress Award was given to Halle Berry for playing an equally-goofy character in the movie "Monster's Ball". I hear that she was paid a lot of money for this movie, perhaps a bonus for having to pretend to have sex with Billy Bob Thornton, which would be enough to make any girl ask for an extra $10 million. But then again, maybe ol Billy Bob has it "going on". After all, he did hang out with Angelina Jolie. I guess women are starting to go for the old, scruffy, stinky look these days. If the short, hairy, semi-attractive relatively nerdy black man look ever comes back in style, I'll have it made.

As a final kicker to "Negro night", a lifetime achievement award was given to Sydney Poitier. On what might normally be a night of great African-American pride, I found myself hanging my face over the toilet. Why has it been so rare since then that a black person has been nominated for these allegedly prestigious awards? Why had it rarely happened before? It was almost as if the Academy was saying "OK, here you go. Take these trophies and don't bother us for another 20 years." It was more of a charity event than anything else, perhaps a quota system, the same found in Corporate America. I was a bit disappointed actually. Usually, racist behavior is much more subtle and sophisticated. Strom Thurmond would have been proud. In light of his black and white checkered past, perhaps he and Billy Bob could put the impregnation of Halle Berry on their joint To-do list.

These image issues are interesting. Our boy Pookie in the election, were his skin the wrong color, would find image getting in the way of his ability to commit a perfectly good crime. These image issues seem to show their nasty heads in nearly everything any of us ever tries to do. I have image issues as a professor, as I witness the blood-curdling cognitive dissonance that takes place when my students see a black guy in the front of the classroom. I mean, I guess I am the first and *only* black professor *they will ever see* for their entire college career. So, the shock is understood and well appreciated.

But the funny thing about the shock that many of us feel when we see a black person in a position that black people are not supposed to be in is that the shock is usually followed by this really weird adjustment. For me, it's almost as if I have to *prove* to some of my students that I am a college professor. I want to say to them, "Hey, I went to a better school than the bearded white guy down the hall." Not that this matters of course, but any veil of legitimacy can be helpful in a given situation. Perhaps I should start keeping my PhD in my pocket, so that I can whip it out like a 12-inch penis, impressing or intimidating any person with the nerve to question the quality of my endowments.

What is made worse is the fact that I am young, not a man that they feel is old enough to have overcome his blackness. I mean, even Michael Jackson had hints of blackness at the age of 32. It took him another 10 years to become a real white man. So, the fact that I have not gone through my complete transformation to an acceptable skin color can create even more hurdles as I explain to students that I am not on the basketball team.

Pookie Bush and the Vietnam War

"I'd rather have them sacrificing on behalf of our nation than, you know, endless hours of testimony on congressional hill." George W. Bush, Fort Meade, Maryland, June 4, 2002

- *76% of the men sent to Vietnam were from lower middle/working class backgrounds.*
- *Total casualties: 58,202*
- *National Guard deaths (where George Bush served): 101*
- *Black men represented 10.6% of Vietnam soldiers, but 12.5% of the casualties, and 14.6% of the non-combat deaths. They were nearly 25% of all casualties in 1968.*
- *During 1967, 64 percent of eligible blacks were drafted, compared with only 31 percent of whites[xvii].*

We don't have to remind ourselves how terrible the Vietnam War was. The thought of going into a dense, hot, unfamiliar jungle, with the possibility that a group of soldiers are going to jump out of nowhere and blow off body parts makes you want to go hide under your bed and crap on yourself. I don't think I've ever gone through anything that intense that wasn't on the other side of a videogame TV screen. In fact, my favorite videogames tend to be those based on combat, so I would surely be fresh meat for the military's videogame advertisements shown in movie theatres: "Hey, join the Army! It's just like playing Play Station" (Fine print at the bottom of the ad: "Except for all the blood and guts and stuff"). On my television, I have shot many "enemies of freedom", and I carry my Uzi like a lumberjack on Viagra, ready to blast any fool that has the nerve step into my path.

I once recall my father telling me about a time when he was nearly robbed. He was getting out of the car with my little brother in a less-than-completely-safe part of town. My brother, being the 14 year old that he was, jumped out of the car to greet his friends. My father paused for a second, noticing a beggar coming toward the car. He also noticed what he thought was a shadow in the bushes, kind of lurking with an "I want to rob you blind" kind of look (you know, the one you get from a good used car salesman). The man also had his hand in his pants. So, either he had to urinate really badly, or he just wanted to keep his finger close to the trigger. Apparently, these robbers had chosen the wrong person to mess with. They obviously don't know my daddy, for whom the word "Violent" is not just a middle name, it is also a nice neck tattoo. The only worse person they could have run across that night would be my mother, who might be considered a cross between Attila the Hun and Jackie Chan. But then again, what dedicated black mother isn't? After running into her, they would have volunteered to come home and scrub the kitchen floor.

My father, the police officer, slowly clenched his gun and waited for the opportunity to blow off the head of someone who might not have been using it very much anyway. Suddenly, in a quick second, the two men made eye contact.

"Larry?" the strange man said.
"Fred, is that you?" my father replied.

The two were friends from long ago, and rather than murdering one another in the street, they chose to embrace. Yes, a touching moment indeed, right out of a ghetto, highly dysfunctional Hallmark card.

My father offered the man a ride to his destination. I have no idea what happened to the man in the bushes, maybe he caught the bus. But the ride alone in the car was a chance for the two men to catch up on the events that had taken place in their lives since their days in Vietnam. I presume that my father knew this guy in a previous life. My father's friend had changed quite a bit since the 1970s. The heroine addiction he brought back from Vietnam had caught up with him, and he spent his days and nights begging for money with his accomplice in the bushes. Of course, his most generous clients usually found themselves with a piece of steal in their ribs, or on their way to a hospital or morgue. I guess that shows how far generosity will get you these days.

As my father described this man to me, I could see his eyes go back to a place I had never been. He was back in the 70s, a time of free love and lots of really interesting and "harmless" drugs. He was also going back to a time when his crack head friend was actually a good man, a church going individual who took care of his family. Something had happened since that time, a life of change and transformation, the kind that takes place when you have gone through things that you spend your life trying to forget.

"You know I was gonna rob yo ass." The man said to my father, as they rode in the car. "I was gonna *kill* yo ass first." My father replied, with a laugh. "What a polite, uplifting exchange!" I thought to myself as my father told me this warped, sick, twisted little story. I sat there with my eyes wider than a 3 car garage, as a kid who clearly had not and did not want to go through whatever it was that these men have experienced that makes them laugh about the fact that they were about to put each other's brains on the sidewalk. The idea of someone scraping my father's childhood memories from the concrete was enough to make me put down my bowl of chitterlings.

The Vietnam War had a major impact on lots of black men and lots of black families. Many men left for this war with the potential to become hard working family men, and came back no good for anyone, either because they were in caskets, their limbs were missing or they were too high to remember what day it was. This of course doesn't apply to all men, but it applies more directly to those men deposited directly into infantry. While one might be tempted to judge them, I am not sure if that's fair. I mean, just the *thought* of being in the Vietnam War makes me want to run for my crack pipe. I am sure that the murdered babies come visit them once a month long after they've moved to the suburbs, and the ability to go from being a government sanctioned mass murderer to a normal American that obeys all laws of society is not exactly like moving down the street. There is an amazing, extremely difficult change you have to go through during war, like forcing Clarence Thomas to be a black man, or asking Condoleeza Rice to actually stand-up for something. The road is a tough one that most Americans will never understand or fully appreciate.

Were Pookie Bush a white man born of privilege, he would surely be able to hide behind such privilege to save his butt. He would be able to run to the National Guard and not even show up for military service during the Vietnam War. The Patriotism card is much cheaper to play when you don't have to spill your blood to prove it. Being a patriotic member of the Bush family might mean putting on a uniform, taking nice pictures and pretending years later that you fought bravely to defend our country. I guess that is how you fend off political contenders who wear their war experience on their foreheads like Nike baseball caps. My favorite is John McCain, who probably mentions his war experience every night at the dinner table. The funny thing is that I am sure that military brass know the pretenders from the real veterans, the guys who've split wigs from the guys who learned to type 60 words a minute. I am sure that during Cabinet meetings to discuss military strategy, Colin Powell is sitting there constantly rubbing his temples to get rid of the pounding headache being caused by the guy in the middle of the room who just learned to spell the word "combat" two days earlier, but still thinks that the word refers to bat semen. Then there are the days when you swear that you just heard him say something like "Combat over here!" or "We are engaged in a series of combatorical strategies in Iraq".

But due to this socioeconomic circumstance, the luck of privilege would not apply to Pookie Bush. Pookie, during the Vietnam Era, may likely have been yet another victim of "Project 100,000", an initiative by the U.S. Government to find 100,000 men who would not quite typically meet the standards for military service. "Not meeting the standard" might mean not meeting the physical requirements, not passing the test, or not graduating from high school. Ultimately, over 300,000 men, 41% of them black, were no longer required to finish high school and exchanged their textbooks and lunch trays for the thrills of infantry fighting in one of the worst wars in U.S. history.

When the nice recruiter for Project 100,000 comes to Pookie's door, he is honored. Not only has he been given an outlet from finishing high school, he is promised by the military and their "bold new initiative" that he will return home with skills that he can use to provide for his family and improve his quality of life. For the first time, his mother will be proud of him. I suppose that we can call this a "Patriot Exchange Program", since Pookie is merely taking the place in infantry of some congressman's son who doesn't have the courage to fight. However, years later, this same son-of-a-congressman will stand tall as

someone who served his country during
wartime.

Of course, if you are a recruiter for the
military, you can't advertise the war as a
place to get your limbs blown off. You also
can't use patriotism as a motive, since you
know good and damn well that black men
had very little to be patriotic about. This
would be especially true in the 60s, where
Pookie knows that he can't even piss in the
same stall as you. Why in the world would
they be patriotic sitting in the back of the
bus? Why would they even BE on the bus
when there is no job to go to? But in spite
of some arguments to the contrary, Pookie,
like many other black men, are
extraordinarily devoted to the military: by
1976, African-American males were 15% of
the new enlistees. But the racism continued,
since they represented only 4% of military
officers[xviii].

The other interesting thing that Pookie
finds out is that although the nice
government man has told him that he is
going to be taught skills to help him after his
military service, it only *seems* that he is
looking for a nice cheap way to find guys to
fight on the front line. He and the other
"beneficiaries" of Project 100,000 find out
that in spite of these promises of additional
job skills, 40% of them are dropped right

into infantry. As the church lady on the TV show Saturday Night Live would say "How conveeeeeeeenient." The idea of duping 18 year olds into doing the things that the old guys are afraid to do themselves is nothing new. It continues with the war in Iraq, where kids are recruited with stupid slogans like "An Army of One". If I were being recruited, I would ask something annoying like "If the Army only has one guy in it, does that mean that I get all the money?", or "What if I am schizophrenic? Does that mean that it is again an Army of Many?" Plus, 18-year olds, even the smart ones, are the easiest targets in the world: they do whatever you say without questioning it. You can send them down hills to die or demand their everlasting loyalty, and they give it to you for an extra 10 bucks. For some reason, the words "Kiss my entire black ass" have not yet entered their vocabularies. These are certainly true American heroes, for you would have to give me half of Bill Gates fortune to get me to go into the battle field to fight for someone else's gas money. Fighting for a noble cause is one thing, but fighting for WD-40 is another.

As some of us know, Pookie Bush has a different Vietnam experience than the one he would have if he were a white boy of privilege. Rather than going AWOL for months at a time, he would actually have to show up. Rather than doing service in the branch of the National Guard that hasn't seen action since the Trojan War, he would be dropped in the middle of the jungle and have to immediately duck to keep from having his ass blown off on the way to the ground. I always thought that the safe and lucky guy in these "jungle drop off" situations was the helicopter pilot. That was the job I wanted. That was until I realized that the pilot is probably the biggest target out there. That's really got to be annoying; you circle off to fly away to safety and someone smacks into you with a missile, or a machine gun bullet comes through the front windshield. I guess that gives new meaning to the term "bad day at the office."

Does Pookie Bush even come home from the war? I don't know. He certainly doesn't have the same chances of coming home as he would if he were the son of a powerful politician opening doors for him to serve in the National Guard. Although African-Americans were only 12% of the population, they represented a quarter of all Vietnam casualties in 1968. In all likelihood, his chances of leaving the military and later running a successful campaign for president are low or none.

Even if you assume that he does make it home, he is not out of the woods yet. I have seen a lot of the "brothers" who made it home from the war, and some of them just "ain't quite right in the head". Again, if I were to go through that kind of experience, I would be writing this book with a straight jacket and a cup full of liquid steak. Like the guy who laughed about blowing my father's brains out, Pookie could have likely ended up as one of the many men who dealt with the horrors of infantry by resorting to "harmless" drugs of the sixties. I recall the stories of older men I know from the war, who would laugh about how you could buy two women and a grocery bag full of marijuana for 5 bucks. Aaah, the good old days! In all seriousness, a black man going to the war had a very different experience from a white man going to war, and the rich had a very different experience from the poor. While coming home mentally and physically healthy *could* happen, no one was surprised if you came home with 3 imaginary friends and a new nickname - "Nubby". If you were waiting for the promise of great and exciting new job opportunities to unfold, you might be better off waiting for Jesus to show up at McDonalds. According to a U.S. government study, 50% of the participants in the Project 100,000 program found that their participation in the program did nothing to help their career prospects[xix]. In fact, the study found that those who never served in the military at all were better off than those who put their body parts on the chopping block........and the survey doesn't even include the dead guys! Pookie would be no exception. He would find himself in the middle of all these statistics.

Most of these stats hit very close to home. As a black person, I rarely meet any other African-American who does not have an uncle, father, or cousin that has had major psychological problems since the Vietnam War. We all have that crazy uncle, the one that shows up to family gatherings and drinks all the beer before the party starts. Perhaps he puts fried chicken in his pocket to save for lunch the next day. You see the grease coming through the jeans and just tell him not to use too much salt. I used to think these men were created by acts of fate, but I realized that it takes an entire system and tragedy on a national scale to create this form of systematic mental illness. It has to be created in large quantities, injected massively, and allowed to be neglected and fester for many decades in a row. It is only then that you can truly watch an entire society of people suffer the effects of something that happened 30 years earlier.

There is no coincidence that since this war, black families have been about as stable as Courtney Love during period week. Is it normal for me to be *surprised* when a family has both a mother and a father? Sadly enough, many of us are. When we see a black family that has all the necessary components, we clap for them, like Halle Berry winning an Oscar. We even have the same pathetic outburst she had on stage. Since when did it become *extraordinary* for a child to have both parents? At the same time, when you have the mental illness and disenfranchisement that exists in the black community, particularly among men from the Vietnam Era, you are not going to get fathers. Instead, you are more likely to get a whole bunch of "baby daddies".

Also, did you ever wonder what is happening to young black males? Why many of them/us are so violent and angry? While this is not always the case, many of us are more likely to identify with the rapper 50-cent than TD Jakes (the blinged out pastor that holds all those dumb Megafest thingies). Perhaps we can look to the missing father, the half father or the crazy father. I know that my personal experience of growing up with a violent, partly crazy father from the Vietnam Era makes me likely to stab you over the last bowl of Cheerios. Even Tiger Woods once mentioned that his father Earl, a Vietnam vet, had the ability to "to slit your throat and then sit down and eat his dinner.[xx]"

Think that the violence of Vietnam dads doesn't affect us? Ever seen Tiger on the golf course? He is as cold and calculated as a paid assassin looking for his mother's killer. I am similar in what I do, but the difference is that we kill you with our skill, not our hands. What is scary is that Tiger and I are the nice ones, and our fathers were the *lucky* guys in Vietnam. Just the fact that they have the sanity to keep a good job and be relatively good people is extraordinary in itself. Many of my friends with fathers from my dad's generation were not so lucky. While it is easy to blame the men or their father's for these problems, you have to think carefully about how difficult it is to go from having your government ask you to blow up 5 year olds to coming home and going to PTA meetings. It ain't so easy my friend, it ain't so easy.

So Pookie, unlike his alter ego Curious George, is part of what I would call the "Real Vietnam generation": The group of men and women who did the most serving of our government and spent the most time getting screwed. Were George to live Pookie's life in Vietnam, it would have likely been a short one.

Why I Would Love to be a White Man

"*And so, in my State of the – my State of the Union – or state – my speech to the nation, whatever you want to call it, speech to the nation – I asked Americans to give 4,000 years – 4,000 hours over the next – the rest of your life – of service to America. That's what I asked – 4,000 hours". George W. Bush, Bridgeport, Conn., April 9, 2002*

- *White median net worth: $43,800*
- *Black median net worth: $3,700*
- *White median household net financial assets: $6,999*
- *Black median household net financial assets: $0[xxi]*

On one of my many lonely, boring nights, I might sometimes wonder to myself, where would I be if I were a white man? How many doors that were closed to me would be open if I did not have so much damn melanin in my skin? I haven't thought about this much, but I have wondered about it just a tiny bit. I remember as a teenager not understanding why white people reacted to me in ways that didn't make sense. It seemed that when I got angry in class or in public, people would get scared. Or, the police would always feel that it was ok to ask me why I was out walking down the street at 1 o'clock in the morning. Was there something wrong with that? Should I have been crawling or flying down the street instead? I also noticed that whenever I got a summer job, I would never get one of those nice, cushy air conditioned jobs where you actually got a chance to *sit down* while working. I always got those greasy, nasty jobs in the back of the restaurant that involved lots of old food and dirty dishes. I would come home every night smelling like 2 day old vomit, as my poor mother would get the thrill of driving home her own personal Puke Boy.

As I perform my current job as a university professor, being white would mean that I would actually have colleagues on my job that look like me. Heck, I would even have colleagues that *like* me. Not that they don't like me, but it sometimes seems that they perceive me as if I am part of an inner city youth program, one that is piloted toward giving those 30-something year old black kids a chance to see what it would be like to teach at a college. Perhaps then I would give up my life of crime and drugs and consider getting an education.

Being one of the youngest in the group of faculty doesn't help either. I get about as much respect as the guy at the end of the bench at the Little League World Series. They smile at me, and then wonder when I am going to go away. I end up keeping to myself, wondering if this is what the House Negroes felt like in the 1800s. You have the best darn job on the plantation, so you don't feel it is necessary to complain, but you feel that the slaves in the field have freedom that you don't have.

I did far more years of graduate school than I care to think about, at far more schools than I care to admit. But in all of

132

these experiences, in all of these different states, in all of these different departments, never once did I have a single black professor. In fact, I almost never had a single black classmate! It would seem that the 1990s would not be the time for our nation to be blazing racial trails. Isn't the year 1997 too late to have a first black *anything?* Every year, I ask my students a simple question "Have you ever had a black professor during your time here at this university?" They sit and stare at me, motionless, like I just asked them if they were wearing underwear. No one moves. Hands sit on the desk, as the girls in the back chomp their gum, and the guys scratch their stomachs.

I then go through the folly each semester of having to "prove" that I am a real professor, not some special effect in a Spiderman movie. I have to do little magic tricks, like complex math calculations off the top of my head, or say things really fast to let them know that I am not just a practical joke. *God forbid I make a mistake,* for that would *truly* show that I am unqualified for my job. The idea that I could have just made a mistake is not a possibility. I am sure that if their dads knew that my school was forcing their kids to learn from black people, they would have asked for a discount on tuition. Not a full refund, just a discount. After all, this is the new millennium.

As a black man who believes in marrying a black woman one day, I can't imagine what it would be like to have a job in which there was a remote possibility of marrying your colleague down the hall. I have only had one black female colleague, and thank God, she found me repulsive. The fact that I have to wonder if "the one black girl in the building" is interested in me makes me think about those poor pandas that are put in a cage and expected to mate: "Ling-ling, he is the only male panda on the entire planet! You haaaave to have sex with him!"

I remember seeing one of my best buddies (who is also black) in a class that I was taking. I had not met him yet, and I can't say he was my best buddy that day, since we didn't know each other. But seeing him across the room actually *scared me.* I am not sure why. Perhaps I was just so used to not seeing other black people that it was a shock to my system, sort of like when a drunk is forced to live off vegetables for 2 weeks. Of course, the drunk eventually adapts to the vegetables and starts to enjoy them. I later found myself slumping in the back of the room right next to my friend every day, as if our joint mathematical prowess was going to protect me from this hostile environment. Then, I thought about it. "Wow, white students get to live like this *all the time.* They get to go to class and find someone to marry. They get to have teachers that look at them and say stupid things like "You remind me of myself when I was your age." There is no way I am going to remind the professor of much of anything other than the guy he just paid to shine his shoes or the one that caused him to walk on the other side of the street on the way to work this morning.

So, needless to say, the idea of having things like mentors, role models and support networks were pretty much out of the question. Instead, I learned to be my own role model and mentor. That's a scary thought, since I am not sure I would make a good mentor for anyone. But then again, if I grow up to become a complete failure, I now have an easily available scapegoat. To further develop my schizophrenic behavior, I thought about who I wanted to be in the future, and I considered that person to be my older brother (I'm not making any of this up, I really am a weirdo). I imitated his actions and took his advice. He gave me support when there was no support coming from anyone or anywhere else. When I found myself in a serious dilemma at the age of 27, I would say "What would Boyce do at the age of 35?" Yeah, that's an issue for Dr. Phil. I'll have to hit him up on his cell phone one day. I am sure that I would get the three beeps and then a message stating "The caller you are trying to reach has said that you are not quite wealthy enough to talk to him. Please check your bank account and don't call back again." In reality, I would say that a trailblazer has to form his own models of success and follow them, sort of like the first guy to make a King Kong movie without really knowing what Kong would look like. That is the method to this deep, disturbing madness.

So, now as a professor, I am the first black teacher I've ever had. I enjoy being in Dr. Watkins' class, for he understands and appreciates me for who I am. He doesn't look at me funny when I come down the hall, and he doesn't ask me if I am at Syracuse on a basketball scholarship. He doesn't hand me his luggage when I walk past him in a fancy hotel, and he doesn't clench his purse when I stand next to him in the elevator. I kind of like having this guy as a teacher, he's waaaay cool.

What I always thought was funny was how you can have so many academic departments at elite universities that have *never* had a black colleague in their presence. This is especially true in my field,

Finance, which is one of the most racist academic fields in the history of all bigot-kind. I'm surprised that they don't make me shine shoes between lectures at academic conferences. I mean, how can an academic department be 150 freakin years old and have *never* had a single black professor? How in the world do you react to that? Do you congratulate them when they finally accomplish this goal, even though it's the year 2021? I mean, my bill collectors never thanked me for payment when I gave them their money back 5 years later. They just gave me an even worse credit rating and told me that I can never have a damn thing from them again. I would be considered a credit risk and technically/officially defined as a "Pathetic Son of a bitch" by the credit rating agencies. Are these "elite" business schools unaware of the handicap they are laying on their students by not allowing them to learn from a diverse set of faculty? How is the Harvard Business School graduate going to react when he meets "Shaniqua Jackson – Vice President of Operations"? Is he going to offer her a nanny's position in his house? Maybe a mistaken identity will lead him to ask her when she plans to be divorced from Bobby Brown.

Remember from what I mentioned earlier: when one sees the glaring lack of diversity which exists in most great

American institutions, there are two conclusions you can come to: 1) either no African-American in the history of this country has ever been qualified to do this job (The Black People are Still Monkeys Theory), or 2) there is a system of racism that excludes certain groups from obtaining this position (The Pricks Blocking the Door Theory). The fact that there are those who conclude that this lack of diversity exists solely due to the incompetence of African Americans makes me want to get on a bus so I can travel across the country and pimp slap each of their mothers.

I am from a good ol state called Kentucky. We are known for a few things, namely: Fried chicken, Louisville sluggers, tobacco, Kentucky bourbon and a horse Derby that is treated as a national holiday. Noting the fact that children are actually excused from school the day before the derby reminds me of why Kentucky is nearly last in the nation in education. No complaints from me though, I hated school anyway, and a horse race is better than English class.

Growing up in this state taught me a lot of important lessons. First, it taught me that every lawyer, doctor or important businessperson is a white man. Secondly, it taught me that anyone who sweeps the floor or picks up the trash is going to be black. Also, anyone who sings, plays basketball or gets arrested for dealing drugs is also going to be black. Those were the roles I was being groomed for, it said so right there on TV, and we all know that if it's on TV, it's *got* to be true. I spent my life being groomed for my place in society, like a man on his wedding day, staring at the 400-pound woman standing at the end of the isle.

The city I grew up in, Louisville, is not much different from any other nameless, medium size city in the U.S. The black kids are not graduating at the same rate as the white kids, the blacks have less money than the whites on average. The black people who feel that they are better than the other black people move to the suburbs. There is one part of town you can go to and wonder if black people even exist anymore, and another part of town where there is one black person for every molecule of oxygen in the sky. This is pretty standard stuff, as black people go out of their way to prove that we can be as snobbish and elitist as everyone else.

In my hometown, there is also what I call "the minority discount". This is a little like racism, but not quite. It's not the kind of racism that makes you feel really bad all at once, like someone calling you nigger on the way to your office. It doesn't cut you like a knife, piercing your lungs and guts along the way. It's a very slow pain, like catching some nasty disease and letting it eat away at your kidneys for the next 35 years. It eventually kills you, but it kills you inside, and it does so nice and slow. What is even crazier is that you don't even realize that you are subjected to it. You just wonder why you subconsciously bow when white people come into your store, or you find little phrases like "Yazza mazza" inexplicably coming out of your mouth when you go to work in the morning. It's kind of like a form of "House Negro Turrets Syndrome".

This minority discount reminds you that black people, while acceptable, are going to be treated just a *little bit* worse than they would if they were white. It might mean that your boss will have a drink with you and call you his buddy, but he would kick your ass if you were to date his daughter. It might mean that when you go into a place of business, they are going to be a little less friendly toward you than if you were white. It might mean that a black teenager is not going to be able to get the comfortable office job answering phones during the summer. That job is preserved for Mindy, the white girl from the suburbs. You just kind of accept this, since you hear things your entire life like "When you are black, don't expect them to treat you the same." So, you don't expect equal treatment, for demanding equality is the quickest way to be called a racist or find your head being pushed through the hood of a police car. There are jokes about those black people who have the audacity to think that they are equal to whites. Most of these jokes are made by other black people. "The boy wouldn't be in trouble if he didn't think he was white," or, "He's white, you're black. That's why YOU were the one who went to jail." I have even heard people say that "OJ Simpson would not have gotten into trouble for murder had he not been messing with those white girls". But then again, maybe they are right. Had he been accused of murdering a black woman, I am not sure if it would have made the local news.

What was most amazing about this minority discount that I experienced in Kentucky is that I didn't even know that it existed until I actually left the state. I thought that *everyone* got treated this way, not just me. Also, I had accepted the facts as presented to me: black people are meant to achieve certain things, but whites were meant to achieve more. The only things we could accomplish that whites could not pretty much existed on the basketball court.

But later, after moving to other states, such as Ohio and New York, I noticed that I was actually a real human being, not one of God's dastardly mistakes. I also no longer had the suspicion that my black skin was due to the fact that I didn't take enough showers.

Don't get me wrong, the other states have their problems. They too are bombarded by images of the media that are less than favorable toward black men. But in the north, there is a level of respect that I received which said "If you are nice to me, then I am probably going to be nice to you". This respect is what kept me from wanting to go back to Kentucky ever again, except to get more fried chicken. So, while I still love the place I was born, you'll be hard pressed to find the word "Kentucky" on my driver's license ever again.

The minority discount I experienced as a youth could have had either one of two effects on me: I could give up, or I could have spent my life irritating as many racist institutions as I could find. I think I did a little bit of both. I certainly did not feel that I was meant to be part of the main stream, for every time I tried to conform to what I thought the world wanted me to be, I always ended up feeling like the hooker who didn't even get the money left on the dresser the next morning. Many middle class African-Americans are in the same boat. We feel like the "good slaves", the ones that work night and day to obtain acceptance from white corporations that are probably never going to give us that promotion that we want to believe we are being considered for. We toil night in and night out, hoping that things have finally changed. But many of us find that although there is more acceptance, we are still known as "the black guy down the hall."

I felt the need to dominate everything I ran into mainly because the chips on my shoulder were bigger than the world trade center. I had something to prove because I had not yet proven it to myself. By going to a predominantly white university and dominating my classmates, I felt that I was actually *showing* them that a black man can be intelligent, motivated, and quite capable of walking circles around their butts. This is hardly a healthy way to keep one's self motivated. The fact that I was so obsessed with the perception that others questioned my intellect was probably driven by the fact that I questioned it myself.

The Big Academic Hustle

"I'm hopeful. I know there is a lot of ambition in Washington, obviously. But I hope the ambitious realize that they are more likely to succeed with success as opposed to failure.", George W. Bush, Interview with the Associated Press, Jan. 18, 2001

- *Proportion of black drivers on I-95 driving through Maryland from January, 1995 through December, 1997 – 17.5%*
- *Proportion of drivers stopped by police that were black – 70%[xxii]*

I went to college at The University of Kentucky. I set to dominate from the time I arrived, primarily because I wanted to irritate those who wanted me to leave. I was surely the student from hell, the one with the black Raiders cap in the front row (Ice Cube taught me to dress that way), answering every question because I had already read the chapter 5 times before class. I even recall having a teacher tell me that if I didn't quit answering so many questions in class, she would *lower* my grade. What? Never before had I ever gotten in trouble for being too prepared for class.

After figuring out the college game, I found myself really angry when I realized the truth: college is just a big hustle. To think that I almost didn't attend because my college counselor told me that I was not "college material" is amazing to me, in light of the fact that I eventually impressed some of the top scholars in the world when going on to earn my PhD. What was even more mind boggling is the fact that some of the great minds of our time have been trapped in the conditions and advice of those who have told them that they are not going to amount to anything. Imagine Einstein picking up your trash every day. Shoot, Einstein might be in a crack house right now! We may be missing out on the chance to have flying automobiles because a great black inventor was told by her idiot counselor that she should go to hair school. The truth is that if you kill a person's mind, you don't have to kill their body, because after that, they are not even going to try.

So, for many guys like me the mind is not used to write computer programs and design cures for diseases, it is instead used to convert ounces to grams or figuring out if you can kill more members of the rival gang with an Uzi or a 9-millimeter. Personally, I like the Uzi, it works better on the Grand Theft Auto videogame. After that, the brilliance is used studying legal books and designing the optimal appeal for an upcoming court date.

College is a hustle for the simple fact that had Pookie Bush been the son of a prominent politician, he would not only be encouraged to go to college, he would have been told to go to Yale, one of the top universities in the world (or so they say). If he came from privilege, he would be told that he has no *choice* but to go on to the 13th

grade, otherwise known as the freshman year.

But Pookie Bush, the poor black kid from the projects, is told that his crack head mother and non-existent father implies that he should spend his life hoping that he can be allowed to fix cars for a living in order to stay out of prison. He is not encouraged to go to the local community college, let alone a school as prestigious as Yale. Ha! To think that someone as incapable as this kid could go to Yale! Why, that's about as likely as an ex-wrestler becoming governor of Minnesota!

During my years in college, I recall sitting with my college counselor discussing graduate school options. He mentioned my high GPA, as if I didn't know that it was already high. He then tried to "help" me by suggesting that I consider "A nice Big Ten school" for graduate education, rather than the Ivy League institution that I had in mind. He seemed to feel, for some reason, that I was not qualified for an Ivy League education. "Why shouldn't I apply? I have a 3.9 GPA on a 4.0 scale. How much better could it get?" I asked him. I knew white students who had gone to Ivy League schools for graduate education, why not me?

He then replied "Well, you could get in on that minority thing, but do you really want to do that?" Part of me often wonders if his reaction to me would have been the same if I had been a blonde-haired white kid. I mean, *someone* has to go to Harvard, Yale and all those other places. Were their GPAs higher than 4.0? Were all my years of hard work discounted because I was going to use the "minority thing"?

After many years of experience as a college professor, I now know that college is, without question, one of the greatest hustles in American history. We convince the less financially endowed, more melanin-endowed students that there is some mystical, high and mighty process that one must go through to get that magical piece of paper. We don't mention the drunken frat boys or the dizzy students who couldn't spell the word "N-B-A". We show pictures of young geniuses wearing flat caps and big, black gowns that make them look like they are about to join the Supreme Court. Those on the outside never learn the hustle because they never get a chance to see inside. Pookie Bush is one of the outsiders, his alter-ego George is invited right in.

As we know, Curious George works his way to graduation at Yale, and although he is not a great student, he is a graduate.

Possessing less ambition and intelligence than a petty thief, he now has the privilege of working with the thieves of Enron, who steal real money, not just watches and wallets. I mean, what good is it to be a thief if you can't take someone's retirement? Were George a black man, his Yale dream would have never lived. And given the fact that Yale admits slightly more African-Americans than the KKK, chances are that any black man, of any intelligence level would be excluded from the big sham of Ivy League education.

Why I Love the School System

"But I also made it clear to (Vladimir Putin) that it's important to think beyond the old days of when we had the concept that if we blew each other up, the world would be safe.", George W. Bush, Washington, D.C. May 1, 2001

- *Percentage of black students in the school system – 12%*
- *Percentage of special education students who are black – 28%[xxiii]*
- *African-Americans are 2.5 times more likely to be defined as "mildly mentally retarded" than their white counterparts[xxiv]*

There are few loves more intense than the one that I have for my old public school system. The system was "systematic" when it came to letting me know things about myself that I would not have otherwise uncovered. It gave me the chance to find out that I have a learning disability and behavior disorder. It gave me the chance to find out that I am not going to amount to anything. It empowered me with the knowledge that my reading, math and intellectual capability were below the norm for my age. In fact, my counselor was nice enough to tell me that I should spend the rest of my life stealing from old people. I would have been very good at that by the way, senior citizens just trust me to death.

I remember two things about high school: the first day I arrived, and the day that I left. I have been meaning to see a therapist about the massive mental block I have when it comes to the 4 years in between. There are days when I can't even say the words "Nineteen eighty-six" without foaming at the mouth. On the last day of school, I recall seeing my English teacher. She was about as evil as any other English teacher with a stick up her butt. I am sure that she didn't need gas money, since riding a broom to work is so much more fuel efficient. The teacher was nice enough to give me my final grade, since I had spent many moons worrying if I was going to pass Senior English. Not that this was anyone's fault but my own. It's kind of tough to pass an English class when you can't even read all the way through the Cliff's Notes. I can, to this day, say that I read at least 40% of the Cliff Note summaries of all the greatest American classics. That's good enough for me to pretend that I am smart when I go to boring cocktail parties: "Canterbury Tales? Yep! That was Chaucer's greatest work!" I would say, as I quickly fill my mouth with a cracker and slip away from the group.

I asked my teacher what my grade was, and she gave me this strange look, like a mother whose child had been found dead in the attic. She said to me, in a slow, falsely empathetic voice, with inverse u-shaped, puppy dog eyes "You got a D-miiiinnnuuuusssss." My frown of concern quickly turned into a vibrant smile. The smile being driven by the fact that summer school was no longer on the agenda.

"Thank you very much." I said to her, as I walked out the door of that school, not looking back. I kept a special bounce in my walk that day, like a guy who just went to Planned Parenthood and found out that the baby wasn't his.

I didn't attend high school graduation. That would be like celebrating the day that black people became slaves. I simply moved forward to my life as an adult with great fear and anticipation. I stepped back into that school twice over the next 15 years: once when I finished college, and again when I became a professor. Walking through those doors, I felt like Jenny, from the Forrest Gump movie, coming back home to the old house in which she was molested. Like Jenny, I wanted to throw rocks through the windows and even burn the place down. I saw this as the place that had stolen my self-esteem and almost kept me from being the person that I was meant to be. I didn't throw rocks at the windows though, and I am sure that some good bleach can wash that urine right out of the wall. But I can say that I was pretty angry, for these walls represented the essence of evil on top of evil, at least for me.

But over the years, my heart lightened up. My second trip was more jovial than the first. It was meant to uplift the spirits of the students, to provide hope and inspiration to those, who like me, were about as enthusiastic as members of a concentration camp. One student asked me if I felt the need to go back to the teachers of the past and say, "I told you so!" I told the student that spending my valuable time going back to make an idiot feel stupid about something they've done would be like telling Don King he has stupid-looking hair. It's not as if they are even going to remember saying those things in the first place, and it's not like they are going to care. Most people, including myself, tend to have amnesia when it comes to the goofy crap that we've done to others. We remember the good stuff. So, I am sure that the teachers who worked hardest to create my demise will stand in line to take credit for my success. I can't blame them. Ask me about something dumb I did 20 years ago, and I am going to assure you that I did the opposite. If a celebrity ever comes and tells me that I once beat him up after school, I am going to swear that I was the kid who shared his lunch with him.

I also remember my mother getting a phone call from my third grade teacher. I am not sure of her name anymore, but I picture her looking a little bit like the Loch Ness Monster, maybe a little shorter. Mrs. Loch Ness had called my mother in to talk about her child. The purpose of the meeting was to give my mother some "educational options" to deal with "children like me." The options involved keeping me in the third grade another year, and pumping me up full of enough drugs to do a remake of "Lady Sings the Blues".

After hearing the words "Hayell naw" from my mother and probably receiving death threats to boot, Mrs. Loch Ness gave up and went home to boil frogs or something. But I wonder to myself: what if I didn't have a mother that was conscientious enough to know that this woman was full of crap? The thought scares me to this day, for by the time I realized that I had been "bamboozled", I would have been strung out like dirty underwear on a laundry wire.

I am sure there is no truth to the scientific studies that cite a connection between adult drug abuse and intense use of child psychiatric medication. I am also sure that the drug companies are being truthful when they say the medications are not addictive, in spite of the fact that they would receive billions of dollars in revenue if they were. I also seriously doubt that the medical community would even *consider* manipulating the definition of the word "addictive" so as to avoid being sued by little Ritalin fiends in their adult years. I just don't believe it.

That is why I love the school system. I found out so many things about myself that I would never have noticed had they not been nice enough to inform me of these facts. I only wonder this: had I been the son of a wealthy politician, would the conversations have been the same?

I Don't Exist, and Neither Does Pookie Bush

"The benefits of helping somebody is beneficial", George W. Bush, April, 2000

158

- *Number of white males murdered per 100,000: 7.3*
- *Number of black males murdered per 100,000: 50.4[xxv]*

Years after finishing high school, I realized something very important. I was not meant to exist. Dr. Watkins is as much of an accident as the actual Boyce Watkins was when his 16-year old mother was looking down at the wrong color on her pregnancy test. The system is not designed for people like me to do anything other than "stay in their place". I was about as expected in my field as Tiger Woods was expected in the country club.

Pookie Bush is not supposed to amount to anything either. Were he born under the right circumstances, then the system would support his existence. But as a young black male, the system has at least 200 ready-made landmines to make sure that accidents don't happen. Pookie becoming President of the United States is *certainly* not an accident that our country would allow to take place. Such events simply do not occur.

What many people do not understand is that it is *not hard* to have bad things happen to you in America when you are a black male. It is *not hard* to get shot, it's not hard to get a horrible education, it's not hard to go to prison, it's incredibly easy to catch AIDS. The list goes on and on. Even living the relatively docile, pathetically boring life I live, I can think of several times in my own life in which I was almost a casualty of many of the issues that affect us all. Some seem to think that if you are black and rich, you have escaped from all this: Those who think this should just ask Kobe Bryant, Michael Jackson, OJ Simpson, Ray Lewis or any other rich black man in America. Some think that if you are highly educated, you have escaped: ask the many pissed off doctors and lawyers who get pulled over by the police every time they turn the key in their BMWs. Ask any aspiring young black student that was stabbed at a wild party on a college campus.

One of the harshest realities that a black kid like Pookie Bush would have to deal with is that survival for the black male in America is not solely about the choices you make. It is just as much about the choices of those around you, many of which are not under your control. I can think of relatives and friends I've had, and Pookie would have these friends also, with whom I could not associate with because they are dealing drugs and could get us both arrested. And many of us have that crazy relative that might get us both shot, or he might be the one doing the shooting. It's like trying to wear a white suit when you are hugging people that jump in mud puddles. These realities don't disappear for me just because my name now has the letters "DR" in front of it. I go back to my community just like everyone else.

Who's to blame for these problems? That is a tough debate. It's hard to discuss this issue without getting into one of the Bill Cosby debates, where you have one side saying "Black people are the ones shooting black people", and the other side saying "Well, it was white people who gave us the gun." I am not sure where Cosby would lie on this argument, but when it comes to issues like this, he needs to go back to the intellectually challenging task of designing new Jello Pudding Pops. The "Pudding Pop" logic is not needed for this kind of issue, since I am like Eddie Murphy, whom in 1982 said that Bill needs to "Have a Coke and a smile and shut the fuck up."

While black people may contribute to the perpetuation of certain cycles, it is difficult to argue that we were the predominant cause of the environment to which we were forced to adapt. I mean, it's not as if I chose to be born in a house with roaches crawling across my eyeballs every night. I also don't think that we chose to castrate ourselves for trying to learn to read, or selling our wives and children so that someone else could get the money for them.

The issue is that these conditions exist, and because we all contributed to the creation of these problems, we are all responsible for fixing them. I will do my part by promising never to murder a black person and not borrowing money from my relatives. Whites can contribute by making sure that they call a white guy "Nigger" every now and then to balance out the use of the "N" word. I mean, if we were all called "niggers", then it wouldn't be such a bad thing. More seriously, perhaps a periodic history lesson might help whites and blacks alike to understand the conditions of the world and how to combat them. This history lesson doesn't mean just watching lots of episodes of the VH-1 show, "I love the 80s". It means really understanding how we ended up in this jacked up situation that we have today.

Given Pookie Bush's intellectual challenges, it is highly unlikely he would survive in the environment presented to today's black male. Were he in a more sheltered environment, he might be OK, sort of like the handicapped monkey that the other monkeys would have left in the forest to die. But the life of a black male is rarely tame or protective. It is one in which the fittest, smartest and strongest are the only ones that survive. But being too fit or too strong might land you in a metal cage. The balancing act is one that most of us are unable to maintain. I've tried balancing for years, but I end up feeling like the guy at the circus who fell off the tightrope, landing on the concrete below.

Moore and Moore Reasons to Watch Who You Be Kickin It With

"I've been to war. I've raised twins. If I had a choice, I'd rather go to war", George W. Bush, Houston Chronicle, January 2002

- *Percentage of white males under the age of 18 below the poverty line: 12.2%*
- *Percentage of black males under the age of 18 below the poverty line: 43.3%[xxvi]*

I spent most of the movie "Fahrenheit 9/11", by Michael Moore as the rest of the nation did, with my jaw mopping up popcorn butter that had been left on the floor. The movie did a rather interesting job undressing the president like a 3-piece suit being ripped off a poorly endowed jellyfish. I was not sure what to expect, since I admit that I am skeptical of any politically biased film. The last thing I wanted to see was a 2-hour infomercial for the Democratic Party. Politics makes me sick, no matter which side of the unbelievably limited two party system you're talking about. Getting a choice of two parties in a political system is kind of yucky to me. It reminds me of eating lunch at school when I could choose between sour kraut or asparagus. The only "freedom" I had back then was to pick the dish that didn't make me puke.

When I see guys like Ralph Nader honestly trying to make a difference, I feel bad for them. After watching the debacle that occurred in the 2000 election, I was also one of the people that would have been tempted to throw rat feces at Nader's head. "The nerve of him to ruin the election for all of us!" I said to myself. I am still saying that sometimes, but then there are days when I simply wish there were a less excruciating way to combat the limited political options created by a two party system. Do I know the answer? Of course not. No one would listen anyway, since the self-interest of politicians rivals that of Satan himself. I am sure that many of them would eat their own children if they could get a few more votes for doing so. I only know that I, like most of America, found myself really choked up watching the 2000 election. The idea that America could be marching down the same path as many countries that have corrupt and immoral political systems is one that makes you want to wet your pants.

During the Moore Infomercial, I found myself actually moved and inspired with the contents of the film. I thought to myself "Deeeyam, this guy really did his work!" I simply loved the way he showed Bush's close ties to the Bin Laden family. What is saddest is that we need a film director to explain to us that having a president and vice president who are former oil company executives could lead to some conflict of interest when going to war with the entire Middle East. Did you NOT think that the gazillions of dollars that the Bush family has earned from the Saudis through the years was going to matter in this conflict? There would be fewer conflicts if OJ Simpson, Marsha Clark and Judge Ito were the same person.

One funny thing about politics is that it's not about right and wrong. It's about interests and agendas. The game is simple: if you are powerful, then your interests and agendas are enforced. If you are weak, then you just get to sit and complain about it. The idealists are the ones who are never elected. The phrase "honest politician" is one that should be banned, for it is usually a lie by definition. I, like much of America, have a lot of respect for former president Bill Clinton. I also, like much of America, have used his nickname "Slick Willy" during cocktail parties. According to a recent interview, Clinton stated that he did not like the name "Slick Willy". I could see why he would not like it. If you are truly slick, then you're not going to say "Yeah, I sho is Slick Willy. I be foolin all yaw, all the time!" No. A true Slick Willy is going to act shocked and appalled that you would refer to him with that name. That is what it means to be truly slick.

Thinking about Bush's interesting links to the Bin Laden family, I wonder what would happen if George's alter-ego,

Pookie, were to have similar kinds of shady characters in his background. If he were to have, say, questionable drug dealers hanging out at The White House. Perhaps he could hire the king pin to run the Drug Enforcement Agency. After all, who would be better to protect the nation from drugs than someone who has sold them, injected them and smoked them personally? Would we be as accepting of these questionable ties if George were black?

For Pookie Bush, the black man, his ties would affect the essence of his existence. Many lawyers, cops, judges and juries are not always quick to figure out exactly who owned the crack that was found in the back seat. For Pookie Bush, the kid without deep pocket parents who can afford a high paying attorney, an association such as the one found with his white alter-ego George during 9/11 would have not only been politically fatal, it could have been physically fatal as well. Whether you are in the street or in the White House, people can see through your bullshit.

I am reminded of when I first became a professor. I had a cousin come see me out of the blue. Seeing him at the door, in the middle of night, uninvited, was not all that comforting to me. But then again, the words "Get the hell off my front porch" might not have been appropriate for the situation. Deep down, I wanted to help family, and I was also curious about how he could have been "just dropping through the neighborhood", given that he lived 500 miles away.

Having this particular relative in my house was one of those things that makes you just want to press the "rewind" button of life. You say to yourself "What was I thinking?" and hope that if you ask God nicely, he will make time go backwards. The details of why this relative was fleeing town are not important, the only important part was that he was fleeing. What was even more important is that during the time he came to visit me, he stole my identity! Yep, changed his name to mine, memorized my resume, and regurgitates my credentials as his own. Jeez, why didn't I think to do that? If I had just stolen someone else's identity, I wouldn't have any student loans! I guess when you have a nation of over 300 million people, nobody really takes note of how many Boyce Watkins' there are at one time.

So, seeing that I now have a twin cousin that I didn't have two years ago, I learned the valuable lesson of the black male: spending your time with questionable characters can get you into a lot of trouble. Given that this is the case for me, one would expect that George Bush's association with the Bin Laden family would have been a super-duper duper whammy. You would expect the entire country to get together on the lawn of the White House, and in conjunction yell "What the hayell?" But nope, it didn't happen. Instead, we sat back and said "Noooo, that can't be possible."

Something else I loved about the Moore Infomercial is the way he showed the Congressional Black Caucus getting "dissed" by The Senate at the beginning of the movie. As they were, one by one, trying to petition against the way the votes were counted in the 2000 Florida election, not one single Senator supported their initiative. The frustration they felt could be seen on their faces, as I am sure that some of them were ready to jump out into the crowd and hand out Congressional Beat-downs. There they stood, looking like the house servants asking their bosses for a day off work. Each time they asked, and each time they were told to go eat watermelon. Moore should have gotten an Oscar for that scene alone. Heck, I might even go buy a fake one and give it to him myself.

What the black congressmen and women felt was no different from the frustration that many so-called well-off blacks have felt through the years, being the silent minority, getting laughed at, ignored and ridiculed like the educated version of the hired help. We might have our PhDs, MDs, JDs, and all the letters in the alphabet, but at times it seems that we are nothing more than Court Jesters. There are days when I say "Man, if I had known it was gonna be like this, I would have stayed at home on the couch!"

The final thrill of the Moore Infomercial was when he lined up the many black males all volunteering to join the military. Apparently, there were few, if any, other opportunities for black males that did not involve picking up trash or getting shot, so these men were looking for new ways to get shot. At least getting "blasted" in Iraq would lead to a more inspirational scene during your final seconds on this earth. I am sure that the digitally-constructed picture of what they would look like with their arms and legs blown off was left out of the recruitment brochure. I wanted to yell through the screen "Don't do it dawg!" But they couldn't hear me, as each of these men lined up for the life of excitement being offered by the U.S. military.

At the same time these black men were lining up to join, Moore went to DC and tried to get many members of Congress to allow their children to enlist to fight in Iraq.

As one would expect, these chickens hurried across the road as if Michael Moore's nickname was Colonel Sanders. Having these politicians confront the reality of their own kids fighting in the war that they so easily sign up for was the funniest thing I've seen since the news story about Rush Limbaugh's drug addiction. Are the drugs the reason Rush lost all that weight? And we all thought it was Tai-bo!

Were Bush a black youth during today's war in Iraq, he would not likely be one of the privileged and protected youths sitting at home as the war was waged overseas. Pookie Bush would be one of the young guys in the ghetto, hoping that fighting in a war would be their chance to make a better life for themselves. How easy it is to be Patriotic when you simply agree with whatever the president wants to do, and hang an American flag on your front porch. I am sure that the degree of patriotism would not be so high if you had to prove it with bullets zipping by your skull as you suck sandy heat down your throat trying to fight for someone else's Texas Tea. Patriotism matters, but in the end, we should figure out who the real patriots are, and pull aside the ones that are willing to use others like pawns on a chess table.

Why Is So Much Being Asked Of Us?

"I appreciate that question because I, in the state of Texas, had heard a lot of discussion about a faith-based initiatives eroding the important bridge between church and state.", George W. Bush, Washington, D.C., Jan. 29, 2001

George Bush arrests uncovered by the media:

- *Hotel theft*
- *Disorderly conduct*
- *Drunken driving*

Amount of time served in jail: none[xxvii]

I've always thought it unfair that we tend to lay all the problems of black people at the doorstep of those who are successful. I am not here to do that to Oprah and the other Money Gods of the black community. I don't expect her to donate her billions toward saving our livelihoods, since her money would not go very far. In spite of the fact that we ask for a lot from people like her, we are asking even more of every day African-Americans. In fact, we are asking them to be Superman.

Think about it like this. According to the book "Black Wealth, White Wealth". There is a strong intergenerational connection between where you are going to end up and where your parents started off. Basically, if your daddy was a poor farmer, then you are most likely going to be a poor farmer too, unless you choose to do something else that is going to make you poor. Either way, you are likely to end up poor. The same is true for white people, black people and green people. Period.

There are some who can overcome the intergenerational parameters that have been set in their lives before they arrive on this earth. They can dodge the gunshots. They can get out of the gang without using a casket. They can learn to read in a school that doesn't have paint on the walls. They can eat their vegetables every day while their mother smokes crack in the bathroom. At the same time, there are those who can overcome the odds in equally amazing, albeit less desirable ways. They can take a 10 million dollar inheritance and end up as trailer trash. They can have a father that is a powerful Hollywood actor, but still end up on death row. Either group of people, the "goodies" and the "baddies" are extraordinary individuals. They are not the ones that sit in the center of the bell curve. They are not going to do average things with their lives, whether they be good or bad. They are going to go from one pole to the other.

With that said, is it logical to expect *everyone in an entire race* to be extraordinary? I mean, you hear it all the time "Well, if Colin Powell can rise from poverty to greatness, then anybody can do it." Isn't that like saying "If I win an

Olympic gold medal in the 100 meter dash, then every member of my family can do it"? Come on granny, get out of your damn wheelchair and stop being such a lazy ass!" Perhaps it was the fact that I won the medal that says that I am *different* from everyone else. If the average person became extraordinary, then extraordinary people would suddenly become average. There would be no bell curve, it would just be a straight line.

The point that we can get from this is that to it seems that perhaps we should consider both nature and nurture when it comes to the outcomes of a group of people. Even someone like George Bush has to be given credit for taking advantage of the ungodly number of opportunities that came his way. But considering the outcome without thinking about the platform is like yelling at a late employee even though he ran to work naked in the snow. The same analysis would have to take place for the son of a sharecropper, attorney, NBA star, or welfare recipient. The expectation that every African-American is going to have super human potential is just plain silly, we don't even have enough Spiderman costumes to go around. We are going to be a distribution of outcomes, whether in wealth, educational attainment, motivation, etc. That is the most that you can expect.

The richest (in terms of income) twenty-five percent of blacks earn one half of the highest 25% of whites. The same is true for the lowest 25%.[xxviii] This is a *distribution* problem, which is more related to systematic biases than to the fact that all black people have just decided to be lazy bums. So, even someone as self-righteous as Bill Cosby would find that he too is a victim of this distribution problem. Relative to how he compares with his black peers, he and Oprah are right up there with Bill Gates. But we all know that Bill Gates has more money than Jesus, and he could probably buy Bill Cosby's mama at a yard sale. Just kidding. You can't buy someone's mama, at least not anymore. But if we matched incomes like a basketball game, where the tallest person on our team guards the tallest person on the other team, Bill Gates would be Shaq, and Bill Cosby would be Mini-me (the little guy from the Austin Powers movie).

This also goes back to the right to be lazy without being extraordinarily penalized for it. The right to be lazy is an important right, just as important as the right to be extraordinary. I am sure that if I were standing next to Dr. Martin Luther King, I would say that my dream is to be able to take a mid afternoon nap next to a white guy and to have people of all races come along and spit on us for being equally pathetic.

That is true equality, and that is what we strive for in America.

OJ Simpson: The Great Exemption

"This case has had full analyzation and has been looked at a lot. I understand the emotionality of death penalty cases."
George W. Bush, June 23, 2000

- *Percentage of whites who feel that OJ Simpson should have been found guilty: 76%*
- *Percentage of non-whites who feel that he should have been found guilty: 47%[xxix]*

Few men have been able to escape their blackness better than the great OJ Simpson. "Juice" can also be called "The Great Juicer", as he was able to extract every black characteristic out of his body and psyche, like a racial juice machine had just sucked him dry. Listening to him in an interview was like listening to Ted Kopple, except maybe a little whiter. He had obtained the love and respect of thousands of fans, white, black and all the other stuff in between.

I would also call OJ "The great Exemption" because it was through his trial that he turned the legal system on its head. He let whites across America know how black people feel when you have to watch someone get away with something that you really think they did. I mean, come on, do you *really* think that we all thought he was innocent? OJ's guilt or innocence was secondary to the broader issue of "sticking it to the man". It's sort of like when you're playing Monopoly with someone who has changed all the rules to their advantage.

181

You then play their rules and find that in order to make their next move, they either have to change the rules again, or cut their own fingers off. Either way, you get to watch them squirm.

I felt that the world really wanted to see OJ go to jail. I wouldn't have lost any sleep over it. But they *couldn't* send him to jail, at least according to the laws that America had created. For the first time in history, the black man was able to use the rules in place to win the game of Monopoly. Do I think OJ killed those people? Hell yes! But if you believe in the American system of justice, you *had* to let him go. Come on: the star witness, Mark Furman, who claimed to have never used the "N" word, was found on tape using the word "Nigger" so many times that even old South plantation owners would have asked him to go to racial sensitivity classes.

The other thing that this trial showed us is that black and white people are on different sides of the psychological spectrum. I was shocked to see the polls and really see how many white people hate me. I thought I saw one poll that said, "75% of all black people think O.J.'s innocent, and 80% of all white people want to hang his mother." I was wondering what the backlash would be, and rarely in my life have I seen so many people cry over someone that they don't even know. In reality, it seemed that all people involved in this case were cartoon characters, cokeheads, and losers. These were the kinds of people that I would not want living next door to me....especially OJ. If he were to come to my house, I would keep a butcher knife in my back pocket: "One false move Juice, and I'm gonna have a juicy carpet!" I would tell him as he came through the front door.

What I also found ironic about this trial was how OJ himself found out how much white people really hate him. Sort of like when your boss calls you the son he never had, until you really try to marry into his family. Suddenly, OJ the white man is replaced by OJ-X, the militant "brotha" who runs back to his community to accept him. I thought it was quite laughable, since OJ had not admitted that he was black since 1968. I wonder if his driver's license even said "Caucasian" on it. But black people are so loving and accepting, we will take anyone back. We take back the Baptist minister who stole all our money. We vote for male presidential candidates with perms in their hair. We even keep the white Jesus picture on the wall, since the new black one would be too expensive. That is what is special about us, we can forgive *anybody.*

Our favorite black male media images:

1) Michael Jordan and Kobe Bryant.

Very cool, tongue-wagging monsters on the ball court. I would shorten my life by 30 years to be Michael Jordan for an hour.

2) Tyrone Doe, the black man on the news getting arrested for only God-knows-what.

Everybody knows Tyrone and his brother Junebug. They are coming soon to a channel near you.

3) The Malcolm X, Kill-Whittie type of brother.

Remember Eddie Murphy reciting, "Kill my landlord" on Saturday Night Live? That was some good stuff, wasn't it?

4) The man running in the direction opposite of where his kids might be.

Kids are cute, who would run away from them? See, it's the child support that might make us run, but not all of us.

5) The successful black man who is "living on the downlow".

He pretends to like women in public, but when women are gone, he strips down to a g-string thong and starts doing his best friend. Sorry Oprah, but that is not all of us, or even half of part of who we are.

6) Bobby Brown, Mike Tyson and the other guys that just can't get it together.

When I see these guys in the media, I want to just give them a big hug. I guess that ruining your life is a great way to get media attention these days.

7) The "Studio-Gangstaz" on BET.

I guess BET stands for "Booties Etcetera". The studio-gangstaz might stab you with a microphone, but most of them don't know how to use a gun.

The Holy Trinity of Black Financial Power

"Do you have blacks, too?" George W. Bush, to Brazilian President Fernando Cardoso, Washington, D.C

Think that the richest African-Americans have achieved equality?

- *Combined net worth of Bill Cosby, Oprah Winfrey and Bob Johnson (the three richest African-Americans) in 2003: $2.9B*
- *Net worth of Bill Gates in 2003: $46B*
- *Bill Gates could spend $2.3M per day for the next 50 years, and still have more money than Cosby, Winfrey and Johnson put together*
- *Assuming Bill Gates does not earn another penny, Oprah Winfrey would have to earn $100M per year for the next 440 years to catch up with him[xxx].*

I have another book forthcoming in which I discuss the impact of people in black leadership and how they affect all of our lives. While there is a horribly short list to choose from, there are those whom I consider to be "The Big Three" when it comes to leadership among black people these days. These are the people that you see on the news every other day, the ones that you bow to in public, and the ones that you hand your first-born child. Like King David, Bob Johnson, Oprah Winfrey and Bill Cosby are the ones that have young mothers reaching out with their kids going "Puleeese take my baby and give him a good home!" If Oprah were a dude, she would have panties being thrown at her by the second. Heck, I might even toss a pair of fruit of the looms, even the clean ones. She is the queen of all queens, the one who "be runnin thangs". She has overcome, overwhelmed and overachieved her way to greatness on television, and now we are all blessed with the chance to learn how to be better soccer moms.

There are others whom you could add to The Holy Trinity of Black Financial Power. Some candidates might be, say, Michael Jordan, or perhaps even Tiger Woods or Russell Simons. Although these guys certainly have wallets bigger than my head, they don't seem to possess the same power as The Big Three. Only Michael Jordan could be a serious contender for this heavy weight of fat-dollar black people. But Michael is about as apolitical as a Buddah statue, so he is not interesting enough to include in such a list anyway.

One thing I can give Michael credit for is at least he has the sense to keep his mouth shut. If you were to ask Michael about any serious political issue, I am sure you would get the same response the police heard on the night Tupac got shot, "Dawg, I ain't seen

NOTHIN!" Michael has to be careful, for running his mouth too much would surely kill his "Miky-Ds" endorsements, and his standing as America's favorite ball boy would surely be tarnished. Some might emphasize the word "boy" in that sentence. I choose to deemphasize the word "ball" or "balls", for some might question if he has any. At least not off the court anyway.

So, it can be said, at the very least, that Oprah has balls. She might point them in the wrong direction and use them to crush black men in the media at the drop of a hat, but she does take stands on issues. I just wish that she didn't always stand on me.

One example might be her episode about "Living on the Down Low", in which she had a black male on the show who wrote a book about some secret culture among black men. Apparently, these men, like Superman, were dressing up as regular guys during the day, and bending over their best friends at night. I am not sure of the details, but it sounded like a pretty sticky situation.

I found it quite interesting and ironic that a woman with such amazing power in the black community would choose such a horrible venue within which to bring black men on her show. I mean, it's not as if we are on her show every week. The pattern is usually the same: there are numerous victims, and black men are almost always considered to be the perpetrators. Isn't that what we also get on the 6 o'clock news?

I admit that I speculate on whether or not Oprah's background as a sexually-abused child has any impact on her vision of black men. I mean, if I had been sexually abused, I might also be tempted to spend my life destroying the public image of everyone who looked like my perpetrator. But there are times when I just want to go on the show and say "Oprah! I didn't do it! I have a freakin alibi!"

After the show, you can imagine the joy I experienced, as I then had to work to convince every woman I know that I really am single, not just pretending to be. I also had to fill out weekly forms explaining why my best friend came to visit in the middle of the night and distribute them to black women on the "Black Women Catchin Brothas on the Downlow" website. That is how they monitor us now, since they want to identify the Vampires early in the process. There is no such website that I know of, but I would not be surprised if there is one out there somewhere. I think I would be more comfortable having John Ashcroft move into my guest bedroom.

I love me some Oprah, but did you ever think that a MIX of black men could be portrayed? Why not show one that actually DIDN'T sleep with the guy next door, or one that DIDN'T cheat on his wife? I would even settle for a guy that has had a job for more than two weeks. I admit that part of me is hurt to see our queen contribute to the destruction of our image in the media. She has used her giant balls to crush and castrate the same men who respect her and try to support her. If I ever have a conversation with Oprah, I will then let her know that I am no longer speaking to her.

Bob Johnson, the founder of BET, is a special one also. I love me some BET, really I do. But each time I turn on the channel, I have to stand at least 10 feet away so that I am not smacked in the head by a thong-laden woman with an enormous booty that is "backing that thang up" into my living room. Don't get me wrong, enormous booties can be a beautiful thing. In fact, I've written congress asking them to make a Big Booty Monument. But I would hope that BET would show at least one video that didn't have 30 close-to-naked women standing around one guy, who is bragging about having had sex with every single one of them. Perhaps Bob Johnson and this guy in the video should get with Oprah and talk to her about how this culture might also be contributing to the spread of venereal disease among young people. This might go farther than just blaming the gay guys.

I love Johnson's rap music videos shown on BET, well at least I used to. But I noticed that black rap music video budgets seem to consist of the following line items:

- *Blingblingables* – Diamond covered watches, expensive cars, Big rented house, fur coats and other crap that a broke-ass rapper can't afford on his first album: $100,000

- *Production crew:* 50 cents

- *Infinite supply of butt-naked women*: priceless.

If you look at videos of other genres, rock and country for example, you don't see the same stuff. Maybe they would have one woman with a bikini, perhaps even 5. But hip-hop artists have set a new standard for the number of women you can have on one set. I mean, the guy has to use a wide-angle lense to get all the booty into the picture!

Before Bob sold out his company, did he oversee any of this? I want to believe that evil demons made him do it. But I am tempted to believe that he gave in to the demons inside; the ones that said to him "Mo money be yo money if you go get ho money".

I was especially surprised when Bob Johnson featured R. Kelly as one of the prize performers at the 2003 BET Music Video Awards. I was sitting there, munching on my food saying to myself, "Isn't R. Kelly the dude that was allegedly just seen on tape having sex with a 14-year old?" But there he was, doing his thing. I can understand supporting the guy, that's what black people do. We are very good at continuing to support people no matter how stupid they are. African-Americans can sometimes be like the beaten down housewife who says to the police, "I just fell officer. I got the black eye when my face hit the door knob at the bottom of the steps." We let them back in, and then they do it again. Our leaders know this. That is why OJ turned black after his trial, so did Michael Jackson. But at least R. Kelly has always been black. Yes, his music has always been perverted and brainless, but he has always been a black brainless pervert.

So, I'm sitting here watching R. Kelly sing another song. I think it was something else having to do with going to the club, getting drunk and having sex afterward with 18 women, something like that. You know, usual R. Kelly stuff. During his performance, I noticed a couple of things: first of all, his performance was longer than the standard. His segment was the last one of the show and lasted several minutes longer than the others, which means that he was something of a keynote performer. Second, they gave him a darn award! I was like "What?"

I mean, I can understand not totally abandoning the guy. I noticed that the Chicago radio stations seemed to let go of their self-righteous ban of R. Kelly songs as soon as he made another hit. I remember R. Kelly during his interview on BET (shortly after the scandal) saying "Just focus on my music. Just focus on my music." Translation: "You idiots, just focus on my music so that you are not tempted to focus on the videotape of me having sex with your daughter. Cause, as soon as I release another hit about getting high and drunk, going to parties and having sex, you are going to forget alllll about it. I'm going to divert your attention the same way the country forgot about the Senator (Gary Condit) accused of killing the intern right before September 11."

So, I can see why Bob Johnson might choose to have R. Kelly on the show. But to give him an award? What the hell is that all about? I think this told me a lot about Bob Johnson. It appears that he is about the Johnson and getting The Johnson all the pleasure that he needs. As long as he has all the women in the world Bobbing for Johnsons, he is going to be a happy camper. I remember him walking out on stage during that show, with two cheerleaders for his new NBA team, the Charlotte Bobcats, one in each arm. He looks out into the crowd and says "Snoop, eat your heart out." Snoop Dog, a great rapper and someone who is not afraid to admit that he doesn't respect women, is also the one with the famous line "I don't love dem hoes". Perhaps he should have saved that line for Bob Johnson.

Bill Cosby is my favorite member of the Black Holy Trinity. He is my boy. The guy with a chin bigger than China, and an ego the size of The Soviet Union. Rarely in my life have I seen someone quite so self-righteous and morally arrogant. I really think he missed his calling as a Catholic Priest, where he could guilt trip people to high heaven and do all his dirty work behind closed doors.

Like everyone else, I loved his show in the 80s and early 90s. The Huxtables were the family that everyone wanted as their own. I personally wanted to be Theo, since Theo got all the girls. He even had girlfriends at my school, just kind of waiting for him in case he ever decided to visit my hometown. At best, I was a Theo replacement, holding his spot until he got there, which fortunately, he never did.

I also sat there in awe as I listened to him chastise "the lower economic peoples" of his own race during the Brown vs. Board of Education 50 year anniversary for the NAACP[xxxi]. During his rant, which was not very Heathcliff Huxtable-like, he basically yelled at black people like we were his illegitimate toddlers, telling us that poor blacks "don't how know to speak", and that we were giving our kids names that sound like "crap". To paraphrase Cosby, "with names like Shaniqua, Taliqua and Mohammed and all of that crap, and all of them are in jail.".

When I heard these comments, I wanted to call the same doctor that worked on Ronald Reagan when he caught Alzheimer's. I would have told the doctor "We got a crazy one at 3 o'clock". I sat there and watched the 67-year old Cosby stand on the stage, with his giant chin flapping and smacking people in the front row, ranting and raving like an eight year old who demands that you give him back his bike. I feel bad going off on Bill Cosby, since that is like beating down your grandfather. But when grand daddy has had too much to drink, somebody needs to whack him a couple of times with a golf club, just to calm his crazy butt down.

I thought "Wow. Our names are crap. So, why don't we just call our kids 'Lil crap-crap' for short?" I also wondered why he would say something like that. Does having a black name mean that you are going to go to jail? Wouldn't the ACLU have something to say about that? I also recall Cosby stating that you can't get a job with a name like that. I thought "Hmm, so if I can't get a job because my name is Shaniqua, would I be able to get a job if my name were Lai-Ming?" Should I be ashamed of having the name "Shaniqua" because it's a bad name to have, or because it is a *black* name?

Well, a 13-year old basically broke things down for Cosby. Kiah Thomas, a young girl who took offense to Cosby's remarks, explained to him that her name doesn't mean "crap". She also explained that she has several friends with the names that he mentioned, and none of them are in jail[xxxii]. There is nothing better than seeing a young kid issue a verbal beat down to a dirty old man. Cosby should be ashamed, for his abuse on the esteem of young people is R Kelly-esque in magnitude. Doesn't he know how hard it already is to get through middle school in your early years? I mean, Fat Albert used to give me comfort as a kid. I didn't need Fat Albert telling me that my name was crap.

You can also compare his comments to those of the Richard Riordan, the State Education Secretary of California. During a reading at an elementary school, a little girl named "Isis" told him that her name was that of an Egyptian Goddess. In response, he told her that her name means "Stupid, dirty girl." I am sure that if Mr. Cosby were there, he might correct him and say, "Sorry Massa, but actually it do mean 'stupid crappy dirty little gal.'"

In another interesting rant, Bill, I mean Dr. Cosby stated something about black people getting shot in the head over a piece of pound cake. Ok, Ok. I know we all like pound cake. I admit that there are times when I, myself would take a couple of bullets over some pound cake. Chocolate icing would make me take the whole clip.

So that I don't confuse the issue, let me give the entire Cosby quote: "These are people going around stealing Coca-Cola. People getting shot in the back of the head over a piece of pound cake and then we run out and we are outraged, [saying] 'The cops shouldn't have shot him.' What the hell was he doing with the pound cake in his hand?" So, effectively, it appears that Mr. Cosby was stating that if you get shot for committing a crime, then you deserve to be shot. So, if you agree that stealing is wrong, then any man caught stealing deserves to be shot in the head. Isn't that a lot like saying that you have the right to cut off your daughter's arm for not doing her homework? After all, we can agree that not doing homework is a bad thing, right? Perhaps someone should make that argument to Bill.

After hearing this quote, I am sure that the entire nation wanted to whack Bill Cosby upside the head with a piece of pound cake. In fact, I could get my ex-girlfriend to make one of her 50-pound pound cakes, since that might put an end to his misery. The misery must be great for him, as he sits at the end of the night reflecting on how dumb he sounds in public. I hate being harsh toward Mr. Cosby, but somebody needs to take down granddaddy, for he has had too much to drink.

Some might say that Cosby's comments were a tad bit elitist. Some might say that he is out of touch. Some might say that he is just getting old and crazy. I would say all of the above, plus an extra two or three descriptors that I choose not to mention. Come on Bill. There has GOT to be a more constructive approach to this problem than attacking the people who are so busy out working that they don't have time to get on stage and beat you down themselves. What's up with that?

I guess to make things better, Cosby then went out and offered to pay for college for a couple of young black kids....again. Hasn't he done that before? What about the Pookie Bush's who will never even get the chance to go to college? Why not find a way to help them? Also, do you really think that Pookie is going to respond to your tirades, as you point the finger at him and compare him to crap because of what his mother named him? Bill Cosby man, you got to chill!

Myths about black men that we all seem to carry

1) We all want to be in the NBA or NFL

Black males are plagued by our athletic gifts. When you don't have other options, the NBA and NFL can call you like mermaids in the ocean. But not everyone wants to do this, and if other options were available, you would no longer find us devoted to one success strategy.

2) We want to rob you every chance we get.

Watching the 6 o'clock news will make you think that we are the biggest criminals in the history of all mankind. I guess we can't look as cool in handcuffs as Kenneth Lay and Martha Stewart.

3) We all like getting high whenever we can.

Drug use happens in all cultures. It's just that we are usually the ones that end up going to jail over it. Not having the money for good attorneys and racial profiling can play a part with this problem. If police pull you over just because of your race, then they are more likely to find out what you've been smoking. After watching the recent actions of the federal government, it's pretty clear that EVERYBODY'S been smoking something.

4) We all want to abandon our kids.

A choice to not be involved may not always be the fault of the male. Not everyone forces himself/herself to deal with the irritations of marriage. I figured out long ago that it would be possible for me to fight with my wife without having to get married to her first.

5) We are not as academically capable as other people.

It takes more intelligence to make it in the street than it does to make it in college. Many of my college students would make it in the street just long enough to get robbed of the welfare check sent to them by their parents.

6) We are all born in poverty

While America has given us plenty of poverty to work with, JJ Evans is not the only black male prototype. Some of us actually do make it out of the projects.

202

7) We are violent and aggressive by nature.

We just act tough a lot of times, but deep down, most of us are good people. But mess with me and I will put a brick upside your head. Just kidding....sort of.

8) We all have rhythm on the dance floor.

I can't dance. Ask my mother. When I dance, people call an ambulance.

9) We all enjoy getting welfare

Welfare is not just a black thing or a poor thing. Anytime you receive income valued greater than the amount of effort used to earn it, you are a welfare recipient. This goes for corporate executives, many college students and the children of millionaires as well. So, there are many rich kids in the city that would make excellent hood rats.

10) We all want to date white women when we are successful.

Nothing makes a black man salivate like a sexy black woman. I am salivating as I write this sentence. But then again, there are some who seem to think that white meat exceeds the quality of dark. There is no reason to judge the package within which love has arrived, but you have to ask yourself if you are only opening certain packages.

Unidentified Black Dudes

"One of the common denominators I have found is that expectations rise above that which is expected.", George W. Bush, Los Angeles, Sept 27, 2000

- *49% of prison inmates are African-American, although they make up 12% of the population*
- *Nearly 1 in 3 black males age 20 – 29 is under some form of criminal justice supervision (prison, probation or parole)*
- *A black male born in 1991 has a 29% chance of spending time in prison at some point in his life[xxxiii]*

One of my favorite TV shows of old was "The Sopranos". Well, actually, it's not "of old". The last I checked, the series was still running and kicking all kinds of butt. I have always wondered how Italians feel about a show that is more laden with stereotypes than an electronics store. But I just accept it blindly, as the rest of America does, watching one Italian whack another one, week after week. It's good stuff, really. At the same time, I've always twinged when watching some guy named Guido shoot at another guy whose name ended with a sound like "idinichi", or something else I couldn't pronounce. I wonder to myself, "What do the Italians think about this?" But I can't lie, the show is great!

There was one particularly interesting episode of "The Sopranos" called "Unidentified Black Males". I found this episode interesting, mainly because I find them all interesting. I sat there watching my big screen TV, the one with enough bass to kill a puppy. The show was good, but I noticed that they had an interesting habit in the show of blaming black men for everything that went wrong. First, there was the part when Tony Soprano was sitting in the office with his psychotherapist and he tells her that his cousin was "pinched" 20 years ago because he was unable to make it to "the spot". She asked him why, and he said something like "A couple of black guys jumped me on the way and robbed me." That turned out to be a lie, since the big fat Tony Soprano had simply fallen on his face after having a panic attack.

The second scene (during the same episode) was when one of the guys decided to beat the crap out of his friend sitting right next to him. These random beatings occur all the time on the show, and you never know why. The guy, worried that the cops might come and get him, gets consolation from another friend as he tells him "I think I just saw two niggers run that way!" (wink wink) I sat there saying to myself, "I didn't see them. Did I miss something on the way to the bathroom?" Of course I was being bamboozled, since there were no black guys, only the imaginary ones they were going to blame for the crime.

The final scene (again, during the same freakin show!) was when Tony Sopranos daughter, Meadow (what a nice, wide-open name. It makes you want to go run through a wheat field, doesn't it?) was telling her boyfriend what happened to her "ex". She said "A couple of black guys shot him in the projects." Again, that was not true. The guy was shot in the back by one of the Italian gangster types so frequently seen on the show. I could testify that this was what happened, since I saw it myself. If I am ever called into court, I am going to tell everything. In fact, I should call Meadow Soprano on the phone and let her know that she is sadly mistaken.

What is the deal with this obsession for blaming black men for every crime against humanity? The only thing that could be worse is if Hitler were black. That would be really cool, wouldn't it? Okay, maybe not. I can't imagine what kind of time THAT brother would get! As Michael Moore argued in his movie "Bowling for Columbine", it does seem that blacks are here for media entertainment for the world. Think about it. When there are, say 50 crimes in a city on a given day, the media gets to choose which crimes to cover. So, they don't HAVE to choose the black guy, they just think that it is going to enhance the ratings. After dealing with the media a great deal myself, I've noticed that *some members* of the media can be *absolute ratings whores*. Though not true for all of them, some will do anything to get their ratings up. I can't blame them, since it is tough to do your newscast from the unemployment office. But being a victim of this race for ratings, I must stand up and take offense. There, I am standing as I write this sentence.

You would think, or at least hope this "blame the black guy" game would stop with the movies. But no such luck. The real world supplies plenty of great examples of "Unidentified Black Dudes" doing some horrible things to other people. We need to find this guy named "Unidentified Black Dudes" and kick his ass. I would be the first in line, wondering why he will not simply "fess up" and take responsibility for what he's done.

Remember Susan Smith? She was the woman in South Carolina who, in 1994, killed her own two kids and then said that a black man did it. I remember feeling bad for this poor woman, I still do. Anybody crazy enough to kill their own kids needs a whole bucket of Prozac, and probably wants to chase it down with a little rat poison. I can't imagine spending those cold, lonely days in prison, while she receives monthly visits from her two kids from beyond the grave. I just hope that it's not true that she killed her kids over a guy, that would give a whole new meaning to the Beyonce song "Crazy in Love".

Then, there is Charles Stewart. In 1990, Stewart decided to kill his pregnant wife. Of course, he also decided that blaming a black man would be more convenient than taking credit for his own accomplishment. And to think that they had just left a child-bearing class? I didn't know that these classes were so stressful. I know pregnant women can be cranky, but shooting your wife might be considered overkill.

Of course once Charles' allegations broke loose, all hell did too. The police were pulling over, searching and stalking every black man like groupies on a chart-topping rapper. They even found a guy that they swore was the perpetrator, and Constitutional rights were tossed aside like an old smelly diaper. Perhaps they felt guilty later when someone discovered that Charles was the one who killed his wife, not the "Unidentified black dudes".

Ever sit and wonder how many people blamed the black guy and *didn't* get caught? I mean, it's not as if all the liars got busted. Ever wonder if there are any men who were arrested for things that they didn't do, mainly because the police were simply looking for somebody to arrest? Ever wonder how this process would have ended in 1848? Do the words "Barbequed Negroes" mean anything to you?

In a 1996 study of DNA exonerations by the Department of Justice, 80% of wrongful convictions were caused by faulty eye-witness testimony[xxxiv]. This faulty testimony might, for example, be someone who saw Michael Jackson commit a crime and then mistakenly told the officer that a black man did it. Or maybe they just thought that the really tanned white guy was tanner than he actually was. I am not here to speculate one way or the other, since I wasn't there. One thing I can say though is that you would like to hope that justice was just, but it seems that justice is for "just us" or "just them", depending on which side of the fence on which you lie. The side on which you lie are going to determine how you are affected by the liars.

The point of all this jabber is that we should be careful about the images we possess of others. These image issues create your first impression before you ever have a chance to say hello. They make people feel that they know you before they see your nametag. They can get you arrested when all you did was get up on the wrong side of the bed.

Pre-existing images and opportunities matter, Bush and others have shown us this. Just the fact that a poor black version of the same person can make you throw up rather than cheer says something about our own internal biases, and how we are quick to misperceive other people. I don't expect that the world is going to love me when I am lazy. I expect them to make fun of me when I am stupid. I expect them to toss me in jail when I act like a bum. I just hope they don't forget to do it just because I am a rich white guy.

About the Author

Dr. Boyce Watkins has presented his message to millions, appearing on the Fox show Hannity & Colmes, USA Today, Forbes Magazine and other national media outlets. He is a Finance Professor at Syracuse University, the first African-American in the history of Syracuse University to ever hold such a post. He is one of only 6 African-American Finance Professors at any of the top 50 business schools. He earned his BA and BS degrees with a nearly perfect GPA and a triple major in Finance, Economics and Business Management from The University of Kentucky. In college, he was selected as Freshman of The Year, the Wall Street Journal Outstanding Graduating Senior and The Lyman T. Johnson Outstanding Graduating Senior. He then went on to earn his Masters Degree in Mathematical Statistics and his Doctorate in Financial Economics, being the only African-American in the United States to earn a PhD in Finance during the year 2002. He does a great deal of public speaking and financial research, and is also the author of *Everything you ever wanted to know about college – A guide for minority students, Quick and dirty secrets of college success,* and *The parental 411 – what every parent should know about their child in college.*

Dr. Watkins lives in New York and spends his semesters writing, teaching and doing research.

Other titles by Dr. Boyce Watkins

www.boycewatkins.com
www.blackmanbush.com

"Everything You Ever Wanted to Know
about College – A Guide for Minority
Students"

"Quick and Dirty Secrets of College Success
– A Professor Tells it All"

"The Parental 411 – What Every Parent
Should Know about Their Child in College"

End Notes

[i] "Neil Bush makes one-day profit over $170,000", Friday, January 2, 2004, *CNN.com*

[ii] "Bush on back foot over corporate past", Thursday July 4, 2002, *guardian.uk*

[iii] "Martha Stewart/Insider Trading : not a "Good Thing", October 22, 2002, *SRImedia.com*

[iv] "Devil May Care" by Tucker Carlson, Talk Magazine, September 1999, p.106

[v] Sorensen and James Marquart, *Prosecutorial and Jury Decision-Making in Post-Furman Texas Capital Cases,* 18 NYU Rev. L & Soc. Ch. 743, 765-72(1990 – 91)

[vi] Common Dreams News Center, 2004

[vii] National Center for Education Statistics, Bureau of Justice Statistics

[viii] The National Center for Education Statistics, 2003 – 2004 report.

[ix] "Black Children Often Mislabelled as Hyperactive in the United States", UNESCO, 2004

[x] ibid

[xi] J.H. Hatfield, "Fortunate Son: George W. Bush and the making of an American President", 2002, Soft Skull Press.

[xii] Drug Policy Alliance, 2001

[xiii] The Sentencing Project, 2001, "Drug policy and the criminal justice system.

[xiv] Oliver, M and Thomas Shapiro, 1995, "Black wealth white wealth"

[xv] ibid

[xvi] Orszag P, and Jonathan Orszag, "A Statistical Analysis of the Palm Beach Vote", 2000.

[xvii] *Encarta Africana*

[xviii] *Encyclopedia of the Vietnam War: A Political, Social, and Military History.* Ed. Spencer C. Tucker. Oxford, UK: ABC-CLIO, 1998

[xix] The American War Library, 1988, "Project 100,000: Testimony and Report on the Study of Vietnam War Era Low Aptitude Military Recruits"
[xx] Sports Illustrated, 1996, "Sportsman of the Year"
[xxi] Oliver, M and Thomas Shapiro, 1995, "Race, Wealth and Inequality in America", *Poverty and Race, November, 1995.*
[xxii] Cole, David, No Equal Justice: Race and Class in the American Criminal Justice System (New York: The New Press, 1999), p. 36.
[xxiii]" Black Children Often Mislabelled as Hyperactive in the United States", UNESCO, Katherine Stapp, April 25, 2000
[xxiv] Oswald, Coutinho, Best and Singh, 1999, *Journal of Special Education*
[xxv] Federal Bureau of Investigation, *Crime in the United States 1995.* Washington, D.C.: U.S. Government Printing Office, 1996
U.S. Bureau of the Census, March 1995
[xxvi] ibid
[xxvii] Michael Moore, online journal.
[xxviii] Oliver, M and Thomas Shapiro, 1995, "Black wealth white wealth"
[xxix] Pollingreport.com survey, May 19 – 20, 1999
[xxx] Forbes Magazine – Richest Americans List, 2003
[xxxi] "Cos and effect: Comedian's remarks spark debate", Newsday.com, July 12, 2004
[xxxii] *The Black Commentator*, Issue 96, June 24, 2004.
[xxxiii] Mauer, Marc "The crisis of the young African-American male and the criminal justice system", 1999, *Report prepared for the U.S. Commission on Civil Rights*
[xxxiv] US Department of Justice, 1996 report.

Printed in the United States
35692LVS00002B/391-444